20 MORE IDEAS

20 MORE IDEAS

IDEAS

FOR TEACHING GIFTED KIDS IN THE MIDDLE SCHOOL & HIGH SCHOOL

EDITED BY
JOEL MCINTOSH

ISBN 1-882664-15-9
Copyright © 1994 by Prufrock Press

Prufrock Press Inc.
P.O. Box 8813
Waco, TX 76714-8813
800-998-2208
http://www.prufrock.com

Table Of Contents

Introduction

If memory serves me, the idea for *The Journal of Secondary Gifted Education* was born during a Sunday afternoon car trip. Just off I-35 between Dallas and Austin, lies Salado, Texas, a little town that boasts lots of antique shops and one of the best restaurants in the state—The Stagecoach Inn (if you go, ask for plenty of hush-puppies). It was to this restaurant that my wife and I were driving (we often took this hour-long trip for Sunday lunch).

As we traveled, we discussed a number of topics. One was a need that I was experiencing as a teacher of secondary gifted children. "There is just so little information and ideas available for secondary teachers of these students," I told my wife. "Of course, when I go to conferences and workshops, there are plenty of teachers doing some wonderful things with their kids, but you can only go to so many conferences. I just wish there were a journal just for teachers of secondary gifted students."

My wife, a magazine editor, smiled and said, "Why don't you and I publish one?" Giving birth to this idea was that simple.

Within a month, we had purchased our first desktop publishing system (a bargain-basement priced, Atari computer). By May of that year, we had lined-up articles for the first issue. In September, our first issue rolled off the press.

The finger crossing worked. Today, *JSGE* acts as the only international journal devoted to secondary teachers of gifted students. Each issue of the journal is read by more than 6,000 teachers in the United States, Canada, and Australia. While our subscriber base has grown, the sophistication of our computer system increased, and our staff made larger, we have never forgotten our original vision—to provide secondary teachers of gifted children with ideas and information they can apply to their classrooms.

This anthology is a chronicle of our first two years. We have included 20 of the more than 60 articles appearing in the journal during that time. Regrettably, some of the earlier articles are not included because they were "lost" in our transition from the Atari desktop publishing system to our present Macintosh system. My hope is that these lost articles might be included in a future edition of this book. Yet, this loss only affects the size of this book, not its present content. The articles included are superb. They are the work of educators across the nation who took their time to share their theories, research, and classroom successes. Their work is at the heart of *JSGE's* success.

—*J.E.M.*

Chapter 1
General Information

Developing Mentorships
For Secondary Students
Guidelines For Teachers And Counselors
At The Middle School And High School

By Jill Reilly, Ed.D.

Arranging mentorships for secondary students takes time and perseverance. At least equally important, finding mentors takes skill in researching possibilities without the aid of a textbook or curriculum and a willingness to depend on the assistance of others. This approach is fundamentally different from planning and executing a lesson taught in class. But, witnessed in the responses of the teachers working with mentoring programs, this approach provides its rewards just as classroom teaching does.

Dr. Dorothy Welch, Mentor Connection teacher for Intermediate District 287, Plymouth, Minnesota, and a teacher for over three decades, describes her experiences as "the most exciting job I've ever had as an educator. It ties together many facets of education to meet students' needs in a meaningful way" (personal communication, February 7, 1991). Mentor program instructor, Elizabeth Jenner, a former Spanish teacher and guidance counselor says this:

> It is the thrill of my heart to connect highly motivated students with top-level professionals. What is inspiring to me is the student, desirous to learn, in face-to-face communication with the mentor, so willing to teach. You can sense the rapport developing almost immediately. Students are so enlivened by being recognized and appreciated by the expert. (personal communication, March 20, 1991)

Despite the differences between classroom instruction coordinating a mentoring program—or, perhaps, because of them—all the teachers I know who are involved with mentoring programs share Welsh's and Jenner's sense of excitement and professional rejuvenation. Initially, however, they also feel uncertain about how to approach the non-classroom part of a mentoring program, finding and developing a mentoring relationship between adults and students. This article provides practical strategies to address the issue of developing mentorships that really work for secondary students and their teachers.

Initiating Contact

Most people find it difficult to approach someone new with a request. For this reason, teachers frequently ask how to approach an initial contact with a prospective mentor.

The Initial Call

Usually the first contact is by telephone. Obviously, the person contacted needs to know who is calling, his or her name, and position. When giving the reason for the call, four points seem most important:

1.   A student has an interest in the professional's field.
2.   The student has exhausted the resources at the school.
3.   The school has an established mentoring program to help meet the student's needs for advanced learning.
4.   The mentoring program is searching for a person who can help this student continue his or her learning in the field.

If the contact indicates an interest to continue the conversation, the instructor can continue with an outline of the nature of the program, specific logistics such as what time students are released from school, what is required of mentors and students, and the mentoring program's role in the endeavor. Prospective mentors seem more comfortable with a course offered through a school for credit than with student inquiries for assistance.

Written Information

After a positive initial response to a telephone conversation, professionals appreciate written information that includes a program description, the reasons mentors are needed, mentor responsibilities, time commitment, and benefits for mentors. The Mentor Program here in Minnesota has developed an introductory brochure for all adults interested in the program and a mentor handbook that provides more in-depth information for initiating a mentorship. If the mentoring program has access to a fax machine, mentors appreciate receiving basic materials while the original conversation is still fresh in their minds.

As prospective mentors become acquainted with the program, their formal training as a mentor has begun. They have received a summary of the program, its goals and objectives, and their possible role within the program. The next step is to make a preliminary assessment of the mentor and mentee match.

Assessing A Prospective Mentor: Traits To Consider

Of course, the first step in arranging a mentorship is to identify people who might have the appropriate expertise. But, there are other considerations as well. Mentors do not always have sufficient time in their schedules to help students carry out a learning project of any length or significance; or, they may not be patient enough to work with young people. Student safety is sometimes an issue, and it is the instructor's responsibility to make sure the mentorship does not place mentees at risk. The next five headings examine these and other concerns.

Technical Expertise

By the time an instructor initiates a mentorship, the student should have a clearly focused topic and preliminary goals for the mentorship. After the instructor has identified an individual who appears to have skill and an interest, it is important to verify that the individual offers the skills that the student specifically needs. This information can be obtained simply by asking about the prospective mentor's business, position, and education or training. If any doubts remain about his or her qualifications, schedule a personal meeting before pursuing a placement for a student.

Time

Prospective mentors need a careful explanation of the time required of them. Students are required to spend a minimum of eight hours per week on their learning, and mentors should allow approximately two hours per week of their own time in preparation. Likewise, mentoring program instructors need to feel comfortable that the mentor and his or her staff will make adequate time to spend with the student. While the mentor's time is a tricky variable to assess, it is worth asking mentors if they believe they can do it. Nothing is more frustrating for mentees than mentors who cannot give the time to keep them learning. The students begin to feel lost in a strange place. They either feel they are wasting time or that they are not worth the time.

Communication Skills

The next question to consider is whether the professional has the personal and instructional skills—and the patience—to communicate information to the student. If the instructor experiences difficulty assessing these skills over the telephone, a face-to-face meeting may be necessary. Sometimes even an initial meeting will not reveal this information.

One enthusiastic and personable prospective mentor sincerely wanted a mentee, yet he tended to over-commit his time and energies. He was late to his first meeting with the mentee and appeared stressed throughout the time they spent together. He canceled the next meeting, and by the third one, the mentee had grown frustrated with the lack of attention and the mentor's inability to make time for her. Ultimately, the mentee and I tactfully suggested that the situation was an additional pressure for him at that time, but perhaps he could mentor another student in the future. He quickly agreed; although, he never initiated communication about his needs. Ending the mentorship was clearly a relief.

Student Safety

Determining whether the mentor will provide a safe atmosphere for learning is another very important criterion. Instructors need to know if the work involves any unusual risks to the student. This requires considerable thought. For example, a student who goes on location with a news reporter might be at risk if required to cover a crime scene or knock on doors to check out the facts of a story. In the laboratory, chemicals, fumes, or power sources are potential dangers. At a veterinarian's office, there is the risk of animal bites. In situations with risk factors, the most important questions to ask potential mentors are if the student will receive safety training and if adequate supervision will be provided.

Additional Considerations

Various sources offer lists of positive traits for mentors in several situations. Haeger and Feldhusen suggest "what to look for in a mentor" who will work with gifted children and adolescents (1986); Boston (1976) also discusses this topic. Flaxman, Asher, and Harrington (1988) consider traits needed to mentor tenacious youth, and Gray

(1988) draws on studies of spontaneous mentoring to suggest traits that ensure successfully planned mentoring programs in businesses. While the priorities just discussed remain foremost, other traits important to consider include the following:

- Is the prospective mentor flexible?
- Does she have good people skills; is she people-oriented? Enthusiastic?
- Is he comfortable with teenagers?
- Is she sensitive to the student's needs and in setting expectations for him?
- Can the mentor generate new questions or research projects for the student to pursue?
- Is he willing and able to help identify potential problems and find solutions for them?
- Can she provide constructive evaluation and feedback to nurture the student's growth?
- Does he perceive possible benefits for the student, business, community, and most importantly, for himself?

Finally, Boston (1976) suggests that the mentor's teaching style match the student's learning style. While all students in our Mentor Program assess their own personal learning styles, it would be very difficult and time-consuming to assess the mentor's teaching style. However, if both student and instructor can clearly explain the student's particular learning needs to a prospective mentor, the mentor will have the opportunity to respond to those needs. Then the instructor can assess the match. The mentor's response to the mentee's needs may reveal all that is necessary for determining whether the match has potential.

For example, some students need to learn in a logical, sequential order, but others require active participation or variety. If Gina wants to actually design a prom gown and the mentor feels that she should only learn design theory, then the match may not be appropriate. However, do not overlook the possibility of negotiation; perhaps the best way for Gina to create her prom gown is to learn the design theory and then apply it to her gown. She can sketch a garment that brings theory into practice. In this way, Gina can learn experientially and still gain the theoretical knowledge necessary to design a gown.

The Initial Mentor Meeting

When the instructor has completed the initial telephone interview and any necessary written exchanges, he or she may choose to schedule a meeting with a potential mentor to further assess the situation or to provide more detailed information. If preliminary questions seem well addressed and the mentor seems agreeable to meeting the student along with the instructor, the instructor may choose to include the student in an initial face-to-face meeting. Before final placement, however, students should always have the opportunity to meet with prospective mentors. Each of the three parties involved—the instructor, student, and prospective mentor—should retain the right to veto pursuing the relationship any further until after the three parties have met and agreed to the terms of the mentorship.

Allowing students an equal say in establishing a mentorship fits with Richardson's (1987) observation of a shift toward greater mentee control in the mentor/mentee selection process. Richardson reports that those involved with youth mentoring believe greater mentee control establishes a relationship more like a spontaneous mentorship. However, no hard data have been derived to determine whether this method is better than matches made solely by program staff.

Zey (1985) suggests that despite the additional effort, it may be advantageous to give participants in a mentor/mentee relationship as much control as possible in the selection process. Boston (1976) concurs stating that mentor and mentee should "select each other in the context of a commitment [to the profession] which is being shaped (in the case of the pupil) or is already formed (in the case of the mentor)" (p. 33).

Establishing Mentorships That Work

The instructor has approved the prospective mentor and the mentor has approved the prospective mentee. The match is in place. Two more factors must be addressed: the logistics of when and where the pair will meet and how they will proceed.

Planning Logistics

With the broad variations in personality and style come a broad range of logistical possibilities for students: When will they meet? Where? How often? For how long? Perhaps the best way to approach meeting arrangements is to allow mentor and student to negotiate it themselves—being certain, of course, that students have allowed ample time in *their* schedules to be able to accommodate the mentors' needs.

For example, Carrie wanted to learn about chemical research, and she had the opportunity for a mentorship with a research chemist employed by a corporation investigating nonlinear optics. Mr. Lyons, her prospective mentor, said that Carrie must spend large blocks of time (four hours minimum) three times weekly in order for her to have sufficient time to master the technical lab skills necessary to observe chemical reactions. Carrie was involved with many activities at her school and hesitated to commit that much time—and to that much driving—but Mr. Lyon's demand was non-negotiable. She agreed to a regular Tuesday, Thursday, and Friday schedule.

In a similar situation, another student opted to decide each week which three afternoons best fit his schedule and allowed him to meet with his mentor. Another student asked to be released from school for one full day each week to learn with Mr. Lyons in his second mentor experience.

Some mentorships demand far less time at the mentor's workplace. For example, a student-writer needed much more time alone to write her play and only one meeting a week to review and evaluate the writing with her mentor. They met each Friday at the mentor's home office or at a restaurant.

Allowing For The Mentor's Perspective

Mentors, of course, view things quite differently than either the course instructor or the student. They want to know the time commitment they and other mentors must make to the student. They wonder about how the commitment will affect their work schedules. We have found that mentors do not want to be involved with disciplinary measures—students who do not report as scheduled, who consistently arrive late, or who do not clean up after themselves. Also, though they willingly write evaluations of students' skills, communications, and work habits, most mentors do not want to determine a letter grade.

Furthermore, mentors, like instructors and students, come in all shapes, sizes, personalities, and teaching styles. Some mentors may want an instructor to actively participate in designing a week-by-week learning plan for the student; or, they may wish to devise their own structured plan independent of the instructor. Other mentors insist that they "go with the flow" of daily events and instruct students as the opportunity arises, not as planned. Therefore, while it is important to establish goals, guidelines, and a "blueprint" or plan for the mentorship, instructors must also allow mentors flexibility in each situation. However, instructors can share several key ideas about mentors' roles with their mentees.

The Mentor's Role

The mentor and pupil are *"servants of tradition,"* Boston (1976) has observed. They "share commitment to the truth of the tradition being communicated" (p. 16). Whether it be the literary tradition, the scientific realm of superconductivity, or the heritage of the filed of human psychology, both mentor and mentee make a moral commitment to the tradition. That commitment is enhanced by the privileged relationship between them. Each relationship will be unique and will require special circumstances suitable to the two parties.

First, and foremost, because of their greater experience, mentors *shape the circumstances* of the learning and the relationship for their mentees. Mentors provide their mentees with the opportunity to learn and time for instruction to take place.

The environment in which the student learns is also very important. Mentors can *shape the environment*, both physical and emotional, to meet the students' needs. Mentors set the emotional tone of the relationship through, for example, their willingness to share information or include mentees. Emotional tone is also conveyed nonverbally through eye contact, tone of voice, and body language, as well as through conversation.

In the physical world, mentors offer mentees access to facilities and equipment that will help their pupils develop. Examples might include a modest work space, an electron microscope, lab equipment, or a priceless collection of original manuscripts and illustrations. Mentors teach from their world to the student.

Mentors *encourage dialogue*. Boston (1976) notes that mentors recapitulate the mentees' experiences. They "focus on the *appropriate* details of feelings and perceptions [of a situation]. What counts is what happened and what the mentor, because of his greater experience and knowledge, knows to be significant" (p. 16). Mentor and mentee exchange ideas about how to most accurately depict a character in a computer game, the appropriate supplies to create a work of art or to frame it, or how to remove a deeply imbedded brain tumor with minimum damage to the surrounding tissue.

Sometimes these challenges also allow the mentor to structure situations that generate problems for the mentee to ponder and suggest original solutions. One helpful process students can use to generate fresh answers is called creative problem solving (Nash & Treffinger, 1986; Feldhusen & Treffinger, 1985). In her book, *Mentoring: A Voiced Scarf*, Noller (1982) described how mentor and mentee can use creative problem solving as they work together.

Mentors *provide regular feedback* to their mentees on all aspects of the mentorship. They clarify the students' questions and their responses. Selecting the appropriate moment for feedback can result in greater strides for the mentee, "the teachable moment." For example, if the mentee is struggling to perfect the design of a pattern for a prom gown, the wise mentor will help the student find a way to solve the problem before calling the student to work on something different. The moment is right to give feedback on the pattern design. Mentors also find ways to regularly evaluate students' progress.

Through their examples, mentors *role model* for their mentees in situations such as courtroom etiquette, buying and selling stocks, restoring an airplane engine, or "sweet-talking" an upset chimpanzee. When mentors share their educational and work backgrounds, they model a path for eager mentees to pursue.

Mentors *role model personal traits* such as a positive attitude, a sound work ethic, steadfast commitment, empathy, risk-taking, flexibility, and communication skills. They can show mentees how to be aware of what is happening around them and to take advantage of opportunities. Mentors can also actively encourage and instruct their mentees in developing these traits.

Mentors *establish connections between other professionals and their mentees*. This results in an invaluable resource to the mentees. It might include simply introducing the mentee to other staff, accompanying a mentee to a professional conference, allowing him to observe a meeting with clients, or requesting an appointment with a colleague who might further develop the mentee's knowledge of an area of mutual interest. Regardless, the professional contacts make by the mentee will be a valued resource in years to come as the mentee enters a professional career. Mentors advocate for their mentees, give advice, and guide them in their learning.

As a mentee noted about her mentor: "She makes me think about things, but never tries to force me ... She treats me with a lot of respect, and I think she realizes the amount of respect I have for her."

Chauvin (1988) says that the role of a mentor can be "a powerful force in leadership development" for youth.

Noller (1982) summarizes the mentor's role through the adage "a guide by the side, not a sage on the stage" (p. 1).

Yes, developing and effective mentorship program on the secondary level takes time and effort, but mentoring relationships are worthwhile for everyone involved.

Jill Reilly, Ed.D., coordinates the Mentor Program for the Dakota County Secondary Technical Center of Intermediate District 917 (Rosemont, Minnesota 55068). Reilly received her doctorate in Educational Leadership from the University of St. Thomas in St. Paul, Minnesota. She is author of Mentorship: The Essential Guide for Schools and Business.

This article is excerpted from Mentorship: The Essential Guide for Schools and Business *with permission from Ohio Psychology Press (1-513-890-7312).*

Works Cited

Boston, B. O. (1976). *The sorcerer's apprentice: A case study in the role of the mentor.* Reston, VA: The Council for Exceptional Children.

Chauvin, J. C. (1988, November/December). Mentoring: A powerful force in leadership development. *G/C/T*, 24-25.

Feldhusen, J. F., & Treffinger, D. J. (1985). *Creative thinking and problem solving in gifted education.* Dubuque, IA: Kendall/Hunt.

Flaxman, I., Asher, C., & Harrington, C. (1988). *Youth mentoring: Programs and practices.* NY: Eric Clearinghouse on Urban Educ.

Gray, W. A. (1988, Summer). Developing a planned mentoring program to facilitate career development. *Career Planning and Adult Development Journal, 4*(2), 9-16.

Hess, K. M. (1984). *Mentor connection first year evaluation report.* Minneapolis: The Educational Cooperative Service Unit of the Twin Cities Area.

Nash, D., & Treffinger, D. (1986). *The mentor.* East Aurora, NY: D.O.K. Publishers.

Noller, R. B. (1982). *Mentoring: A voiced scarf.* Buffalo, NY: Bearly Limited.

Richardson, H. P. (1987). Student mentoring: A collaborative approach to the school dropout problem. In W. A. Gray & M. M. Gray (Eds.). *Mentoring: Aid to excellence in education, the family, and the community.* Proceedings of the First International Conference on Mentoring (Vol. I). Vancouver, BC: Internat'l Assn. for Mentoring.

Zey, M. G. (1985, February). Mentor programs: Making the right moves. *Personnel Journal, 64*(2), 53-57.

Changing Attitudes
Attitudes Make the Difference
In Secondary Gifted Education

By Marsha J. Stephenson

Attitudes of administrators, teachers, counselors, parents, and the gifted students themselves can either make or break the secondary experience of gifted children. The separate, yet congruent, roles of all five participants must focus on one major goal: a successful, enlightening, challenging, rewarding, expanding education for the gifted student at the secondary level.

Although strides have been taken to promote gifted education, all too often gifted education begins in the elementary grades—where it should—but ends as a student enters the secondary system, and, "Contrary to popular opinion, the gifted do not ordinarily excel (or realize their potential) without assistance," says Jeanette Parker whose studies have shown that at least 17.6% of gifted youth drop out of high school (1988). The loss of potential for advanced education and leadership from these students has a dramatic effect on our society. As with all gifted students, these dropout gifted students are capable of complex thinking and handling complex issues which our society presently faces, and will face, in the future (Parker, 1988). Parker states that if democratic education means education appropriate for the child, then differentiated education for the gifted must be mandatory (1988), and this differentiated education must not stop in secondary schools.

The Administrators

Yet, as Barbara Clark states in her book *Growing Up Gifted,* "The largest barrier [to secondary programs] is the perception that program modification for gifted students is unnecessary in secondary school" (1988). Therefore, the first attitude which must be addressed is the attitude of school administrators—those people who control the programs in the first place within the school system.

Because administrators should have the total picture with which to work, they must have information in their hands which shows that gifted students need comprehensive special programs. Administrators must sell their proposals to superintendents, school boards, and the community. Those in charge must have the facts. Frequently, the system's attitudes toward gifted education are not negative as much as neutral. The gifted are seen as only a small fraction of the overall system, and this fraction seems to need little assistance because the wheel does not seem to be squeaking very loudly. This attitude of neutrality, or negativism, if the attitude is indeed negative, must be addressed through the grease of knowledge and advocacy. The students must have a commitment from the system before any program can begin, much less mature!

Having a commitment to gifted education does not guarantee a successful gifted program, though. The research done by Thistlewaite in 1958, showed that 45% of secondary gifted programs were either "inadequate" or had "specific defects" (Clark, 1988). Clark says her research shows that, if anything, gifted programs today are at a lower percentage of serving the intended students adequately than they were in past years (1988).

Administrators need to know the facts about effective programming for the gifted learner. Traditional school program planning cannot adequately provide for the atypical developmental needs of the gifted and talented according to Mary Landrum (1987). Gifted education on the secondary level must be differentiated for the gifted (Clark, 1988). This can be accomplished most successfully when gifted students are with gifted peers—not mainstreamed. Mainstreaming gifted students causes a lack of challenge and results in boredom (Clark, 1983; Davis & Rimm, 1985; Chapman & McAlpine, 1988), eventually ending in a loss to the system of more gifted students. Further, Chapman and McAlpine found that in a mainstream situation "gifted ... students' academic self-concepts may have levelled off in line with the maintenance of performance ranking in school" (1988). In other words, the student does what is necessary to be at the top or get the top score or grade in a less challenging class, and no more. In a study done by Bogie and Buckhalt, gifted students credit their achievement to low levels of task difficulty and not to their abilities (1987). Clark says gifted students want separate classes. They need to be with other students who have the same thought processes and similar personal problems. When a non-gifted student asks a gifted student where he or she got the idea he or she has just presented to the class, and the presenting student has simply done it intuitively—i.e. through his or her own synaptic thought process (which is different than a non-gifted student's process), it is impossible to explain to the non-gifted student how this thought process occurs. Both students end up feeling out of place. However, other gifted students understand the process because they too think this way.

Studies show that gifted students nurtured in G/T classes do better all around than those who are mainstreamed (Clark 1988). Further, claims that the gifted are needed in mainstreamed classrooms because these students act as models for others is not supported by research. Feldhusen says that gifted students are *not* models for other students, although he says proponents for mainstreaming gifted students say they are. Feldhusen says studies by Schunk in 1987 prove that "children model on other children who are of similar ability to themselves and who are coping well with school, and children of low and average ability do not model themselves on fast learners" (1989). Feldhusen refers to another study, one researched by Nichols and Miller, in which it was shown that "for less able children the comparisons may be debilitating or devastating when they are confronted in the classroom day after day by the superior performance of gifted learners" (1989).

The Teachers

Gifted students also need to be in a class which, instead of being simply labeled "gifted" and merely accelerated, involves content seen in a different light or from a different angle. The attitude of teachers makes the difference in understanding and presenting these different lights and angles. Such differentiating, which is essential to the learning process of the gifted, means matching the teaching style to the learning style of the gifted student. Parker refers back to Piaget who explained that "extensive opportunities for social interaction within the classroom (not often feasible within a traditional classroom setting) can enable the gifted child to relinquish the egocentricism so often cited as a problem of the intellectually or creatively superior student" (1988). This kind of classroom setting must be facilitated by a teacher who knows about and understands gifted students and differentiation.

Lundrum says gifted programs and children need someone in a position of authority in the school who knows and understands gifted children and their emotional as well as educational needs (1987). Students appreciate teachers who understand them and who are concerned about how the gifted student feels (Clark, 1988). The teacher who revels in the thought of being able to "trap" a gifted student or make an exam so hard that the student will "finally" fail or make a "B," should *not* be a teacher of the gifted. "Research on bright underachievers reveals that the teacher's attitude is important in shaping gifted students' motivation toward achievement" (Leroux, 1988). Facilitators for the gifted must be "prepared, purposeful, disciplined, and caring helpers who are committed to their work with the gifted" (Kenny, 1986). The teacher must have a "special sensitivity to emotional problems of the gifted adolescent" (Kaiser & Berndt, 1985). Special training in gifted education is extremely important to those who work with gifted students, but in the final analysis, the caring, understanding, and commitment to gifted students must be there before it can be trained.

As Culross and Jenkins-Friedman explain, one of the greatest personality traits that a facilitator of the gifted can possess is a sense of humor (1988). Gifted students have the weight of the world on their shoulders; hence, they need to understand, as Oscar Wilde said, "Life is too important to be taken seriously." With humor, the gifted classroom comes alive and remains exciting or pleasantly bearable even in the worst of times!

The teacher in the gifted secondary program is not just working with a transference of a body of knowledge in a content area, but rather is working with a program which deals with the whole child; a program which realizes the totality of the gifted student.

The Students

The dynamic of the teacher and her students encompasses more than just the individual teacher and students in a given classroom situation. The students bring with them each day their association with their families, perhaps the most important external aspect to their success. In a timely article written by Brian O'Reilly in *Fortune* magazine (January 1, 1990) the comment is made that "The most important thing a parent can do for a child is encourage a high sense of self-esteem." The author continues by explaining that "kids who have a sense of self-worth flourish." Cornell and Grooseberg's studies show that supportive and open family relationships are extremely important to a child's self-esteem (1987). They found that the student's adjustment in life is more readily assisted by a family which interacts "cooperatively, with minimal conflict and maximum freedom for personal expression" (1987). This family support gives them a "safe-haven"—a place where they do not have to confront the world but can breath, relax, and regroup their thoughts, composure, and strength. The students survive because of the family's positive attitude.

If the students do not have this support, they soon tire, wear down, and become vulnerable. They are concerned with their own lives, and they are empirically concerned with global issues, yet they often feel helpless to do anything about it (Delisle, 1986). The gifted adolescents themselves reported that this "degree of loneliness" they feel is "a function of anger, depression, and stressful life changes" (Kaiser & Berndt, 1985). The world of answers they see is too often alcohol, drugs, and even suicide—a radical step, but an undeniably possible one. But, the gifted students who have the support of significant adults and peers will be able to cope and indeed flourish because they can find alternatives (Delisle, 1986).

The Counselors

Obviously, gifted students need help and guidance just like any other person. The difference between gifted students and non-gifted students is the kind of problems they face and the way in which they look at the problems and at themselves (Landrum, 1987).

Counselors who understand the gifted are part of the gifted team since the counselor has access to support systems in emotional and vocational areas which are usually not accessible to the others. Blackburn and Erickson (1986), Clark (1988), and Landrum (1987) all give extended examples of what kinds of guidance and counseling are necessary for the gifted. No matter what individual counseling formulas are offered, they all encompass the use of parents, school staff, counselors, and the student in an over-arching and comprehensive program. Therefore, to be able to reach the students in all facets of their complex lives, to be able to serve these students and help them to become producers of knowledge—of which they are totally capable—all those who touch their lives each day must be part of a comprehensive education and counseling program which looks at the gifted students with attitudes of acceptance, encouragement, and understanding.

From the parent, whose first function in the guidance/counseling system for the gifted child is to enhance the school-home relationship (Landrum, 1987); to the counselor, whose part is to continue to enhance the school-home relationship; to the teacher, whose job is to help design and implement the formal educational program; to the administrators, whose function is to keep the programs open and viable; all must work in unison toward the one goal of helping the gifted student in every way possible. Gifted students are not better, only different; and if this difference is going to make a difference, it must be allowed to exist and grow because all mankind will benefit from the knowledge these gifted people produce.

Marsha Stephenson is currently an adjunct professor at Southwest Texas State University and an English Honors and Advanced Placement teacher at Pflugerville High School, Pflugerville, Texas 78728. She is also a doctoral student at Baylor University, Waco, Texas 76798.

Works Cited

Blackburn, A.C., & Erickson, D.B. (1986). "Predictable crises of the gifted student." *Journal of Counseling and Development*, 64, 552-555.

Bogie, C.E., & Buckhalt, J.A. (1987). "Reactions to failure and success among gifted, average, and EMR students." *Gifted Child Quarterly*, 31, 70-78.

Chapman, J.W., & McAlpine, D.D. (1988). "Student's perception of ability." *Gifted Child Quarterly*, 32, 222-225.

Clark, B. (1988). *Growing up gifted*. Columbus: Merrill.

Cornell, D.G., & Grossberg, I. W. (1987). "Family environment and personality adjustment in gifted program children." *Gifted Child Quarterly*, 31, 59-64.

Culross, R.R., & Jenkins-Friedman, R. (1988). "On coping and defending: Applying Bruner's personal growth principals to working with gifted/talented students." *Gifted Child Quarterly*, 32, 261-266.

Delisle, J.R. (1986). "Death with honors: Suicide among gifted adolescents." *Journal of Counseling and Development*, 64, 558-560.

Feldhusen, J.F. (1988). "Why the public schools will continue to neglect the gifted." *Gifted Child Today*, 61(12), 55-59.

Kaiser, C.F., Berndt, D.J. (1985). "Predictors of loneliness in the gifted adolescent." *Gifted Child Quarterly*, 29, 74-77.

Kenny, A. (1986). "The helping relationship." *Gifted Child Today*, 9(5), 41-43.

Landrum, M.S. (1987). "Guidelines for implementing a guidance/counseling program for gifted and talented students." *Roeper Review*, 10(2), 103-107.

Leroux, J.A. (1988). "Voices from the classroom: Academic and social self-concepts of gifted adolescents." *Journal for the Education of the Gifted*, 11(3), 3-18.

O'Reilly, B. (1990). "Why grade 'A' execs get an 'F' as parents." *Fortune*, pp. 36-46.

Parker, J. (1988). "Differentiated programs for the G/C/T: Luxury or necessity?" *Gifted Child Today*, 47(9), 31-33.

Idea Checklists
An Idea Checklist Is An Effective Strategy
For Helping Students Develop Ideas

By Joel E. McIntosh

One of the most challenging aspects of a teacher's job is helping students develop original insights into the concepts and generalizations they study. One strategy for helping students develop such insights is brainstorming—a strategy with which many teachers are familiar. Yet, there are many others. This article focuses on one such strategy, the idea checklist. Alex Osborn (1957) proposes the idea checklist as an excellent tool for helping students generate new ideas. Essentially, an idea checklist is a list of items which students use to "spur" them on to new insight. For example, if a class were discussing possible characters for a story they are to write, the teacher might ask if the idea of "glass" brings to mind a character. This idea might suggest to students the skipper of a glass-bottom boat or a glass-maker of the Victorian age. If the teacher then suggested a "match," students might think of a firefighter or a girl with a twin (a match).

Idea checklists are easy to create. For example, I created the idea checklist used in the first activity below by randomly opening the yellow pages of a phone book and looking at the headings. I created the idea checklist for the second activity by considering what places one might find teenagers today.

The third activity is slightly different than the first two. In it, students work with a type of idea checklist proposed by Osborn (1957) and adapted by Eberle (1989) called SCAMPER. The SCAMPER checklist offers a structured way to manipulate the way students view a question, issue, or object. Manipulating one's view often generates new and original insight. SCAMPER is an acronym for the following:

- **Substitute**—A new idea or item is substituted for an idea or item proposed earlier in the idea generating session. For example, if students are examining ways a classroom might be made more attractive, a student might suggest brightening the room with fresh, potted flowers. The teacher might ask a substitution question by saying, "What are some other things [substitute] we might put in a pot which would brighten the room?" A student might answer, "We could grow herbs which would make the room smell better."

- **Combine**—Students combine two or more ideas generated earlier to create an altogether new idea. For example, the students considering ways to improve the classroom might be asked if there is a way to combine their fresh, potted flower idea and an earlier idea that brighter colors could be used on the bulletin boards. One student might suggest that a bulletin board of many flowers be created—each student could bring in a favorite flower to be pressed, labeled, and pinned to one of the bulletin boards in the classroom.
- **Adapt**—An idea generated earlier is adapted or adjusted. For instance, one student might suggest that the bulletin board of many flowers mentioned above, could be made even more interesting if the space between the board's base and the floor were decorated [adapted] with construction paper so that it looked like a pot. Then the class could draw stems from each of the flowers to the pot. The result would be a board that looked like a huge flower pot.
- **Modify, Magnify, and Minify**—Ideas are changed so that they become modified, magnified, or minified. For example, in the case of magnifying an idea, a class discussing ways to improve a classroom might be asked, "What are some ways we could make the room look larger [magnify]?" One student might suggest that the rows of desks be replaced with large circular tables. These circular tables would allow for more open space that would make the room seem larger.
- **Put to other uses**—Students examine items or ideas to see if they could serve other purposes. For instance, one student might look at a section of unused bookcase space and suggest that it be used as a display case for exceptional student products.
- **Eliminate**—Students eliminate items or objects and suggest alternatives to fill the gap. For example, in the classroom improvement session, the teacher might suggest that all the desks in the room be eliminated. The teacher would then ask students to suggest ideas for filling the gap left by the removed desks. One student might suggest throw pillows or bean-bag chairs, another might suggest two long tables for writing, and another student might suggest the installation of two computer centers.
- **Reverse or Rearrange**—Students reverse a sequence within an idea or change a pattern within the idea. In our classroom improvement example, students might suggest that the rows of desks be broken down [rearranged] into many circular groups of desks or that all the desks be rearranged in a large circle.

Whether you choose to use SCAMPER or simply a random list of items, the idea checklist has plenty of possible applications to classroom content. On the elementary level, the idea checklist can be used in social studies to help students choose possible occupations to research (using a checklist to identify categories under which more specific occupations might occur), in science to help students generate a group of items which can be used in an experiment to test magnetic attractiveness (using a checklist to identify items which might not be commonly found in the classroom), or in language arts to help students write a new ending to a story (using a checklist to develop possible situations which might occur in the new ending).

On the secondary level, the idea checklist can be used to help students develop a creative short story (using a checklist to generate characters, plots, settings, and conflicts for a story), help design an independent study unit about London in the 1600s (using a checklist to generate questions about the city during that period), or generate a list of alternative energy sources (first using a checklist to identify various forms of energy found about us).

Joel McIntosh is currently the publisher of The Journal of Secondary Gifted Education, Gifted Child Today, *and* Creative Kids *in Waco, Texas 76710.*

Works Cited

Eberle, R. (1971). Scamper: games for imagination development. Buffalo: D.O.K.

Osborn, A. (1957). Applied imagination. New York: Charles Scribners Sons.

This article was excerpted from
Creative Problem Solving in the Classroom (1991)
by Joel E. McIntosh and April W. Meacham,
Waco, TX: Prufrock Press.

Idea Checklist Activity 1
(Non-Discipline Specific)

Summer Vacation

Over the last six years, you and your classmates have raised money through sales of candy, sales of magazine subscriptions, and book fairs. It is now time to spend all of that money, and your class has decided to spend it on a class retreat—a week-long vacation together.

The student council has asked for lists of possible vacation ideas. To help create a list of unique ideas, the council has provided an idea checklist—a list of items that can help you generate new ideas. For example, in the list below, the word "Guitars" appears. This word might make you think of singers with guitars like George Strait, and you know that many of your friends like to listen to country-and-western singers like Strait. To see such singers in concert, you might suggest that your class travel to the Grand Old Opry in Nashville, Tennessee. You would list "Grand Old Opry & Nashville, Tennessee" below next to the word "Guitars."

Idea checklists are easy to create. The one below was created by randomly opening the yellow pages of a phone book and looking at the headings.

Boats: Pests:

Farms: Pizza:

Glass: Veterinarians:

Guitars: Magic:

Idea Checklist Activity 2
(Discipline: Language Arts)

Huckleberry Finn Again

Huckleberry Finn is the embodiment of a character type in the American culture—a mixture of both innocence and experience. The activity below will act as a pre-writing step in the writing process. It will help you develop a story line for a short story you will write in which Huck Finn finds himself in an unusual situation. Consider the many different ways Huck might react to the various settings listed below.

For each setting, describe in two or three sentences what you believe Huck's reaction might be to the listed setting. Consider the details he would notice, the feelings he would have, and analogous situations from the novel that might support your ideas.

An English class in a modern American high school:

Lunch at a McDonald's Restaurant:

A video arcade in a modern shopping mall:

A teen dance club:

Idea Checklist Activity 3 (Secondary)

SCAMPER

SCAMPER is a type of idea checklist in which ideas are substituted, combined, adapted, modified, magnified, minified, put to other uses, eliminated, and rearranged. In the activity below, the SCAMPER technique is used to create questions that ask you to view the issue of life after high school in many different ways.

Exploring your desires, interests, and speculations about your options after high school can be helpful in making your future plans. In this activity, you will use divergent thinking to consider your life after high school. Simply answer the questions below. Remember, wild ideas are acceptable.

1. What occupational and educational advantages might a city with more than 100,000 people offer over a much smaller city? [Magnify]

2. In what ways might going to a small college, rather than a large one, make it easier for you to make friends? In what ways might it be harder? [Minify]

3. What purposes, other than those which are strictly social or academic, do you think going to college serves? [Put to other uses]

_____

_____

_____

_____

4. What are some ways of furthering your education after high school that do not include going to a university? [Substitute]

_____

_____

_____

_____

5. What are some ways you might combine your occupation and education? [Combine]

_____

_____

_____

_____

6. What are some of the advantages and disadvantages to beginning your career before getting a college education? [Rearrange]

_____

_____

_____

_____

7. If your parents informed you that they would be unable to support you in any way after your high school graduation, in what ways might your plans be changed? [Eliminate]

_____

_____

_____

_____

_____

_____

Career Exploration For The
Middle School Classroom

By Karen Renner

C areer education is one of the more important aspects in an effective program of gifted education (Clendening, 1980). Gifted students, perhaps more than average students, require a program that focuses on the development of their special skills and abilities in order to attain their goals (Hirt, 1990). Knowing how important career education is for the gifted, a co-worker and I developed a six-week unit on career education for our eighth grade gifted students.

The gifted and talented students in my junior high school are served in an advanced English class with the English teacher and counselor working as a team. We plan units of study that include research, problem-solving and independent study as well as developing strong writing skills and meeting the state requirements for mastery of eighth grade English. The career unit that we developed two years ago includes all of the above aspects.

There are several reasons that career planning is appropriate for gifted/talented eighth grade students in our school. During the second semester, eighth graders pre-register for high school. We felt that if these gifted students had an idea of the requirements for different careers, they would be better able to plan a four-year course of study that would benefit their future plans.

A second reason for offering career education is that our gifted/talented students often have unrealistic expectations for their futures. School work is usually easy for these students, so they expect that life will also be easy for them. Several of our students thought that after graduating from college they would find $100,000-a-year chief executive positions with all possible benefits. They never thought that they would have to start at the bottom and work their way up the ladder. Many gifted students have unrealistically high expectations of their abilities and also feel that their parents have high expectations for them. While setting high goals is very admirable, these students need to realize that there are many professions that require an early life-long commitment (Hirt, 1990).

A third reason for a unit on career education is that our gifted students are interested in so many different subjects and often have talents in so many different areas that they have great difficulty in choosing one interest or talent to develop. The opportunity to research and explore different career choices gives these students a chance to identify one or two areas where their talents, interests, and a career choice match.

A fourth reason for having eighth grade students study careers is that they are also required to explore some colleges or universities. They must research the cost of four years of college, entrance requirements, and scholarship opportunities.

Most are shocked at the cost of four years of undergraduate education and the level of competition for scholarships and grants. They begin to realize that what they do their freshman year of high school is just as important to their future as their senior year. They also note that colleges look at extracurricular activities as well as academic standing.

Our career unit incorporates the following:

1. Research on college and career choices.
2. Interviewing professionals in careers chosen by the students.
3. Producing and publishing a brochure suitable for placement in the school library.

The following activities are listed in the order that works for our situation. However, we have learned that flexibility in scheduling and rescheduling activities is a vital requirement for us as teachers of the gifted.

Activity 1

The school counselor comes to the class and administers the *Job-O Career Planning Inventory*. This takes two days and gives students career choices that match some of their interests. The students choose the career in which they are most interested and write to a university or a trade/technical school for a catalog. It has been our experience that the schools respond in one or two weeks so the letter-writing activity is scheduled about two weeks before we plan to start the unit.

Activity 2

The students choose a professional in their chosen career and write a letter inviting that person to come speak to the class. The students must be very specific about dates, times, and questions that they want to have answered. We have also learned to set a specific date for a response.

Since we live in a small rural town, we sometimes rely on professors from a nearby university or professional people in related areas to speak to the students. For example, a student who was interested in robotics invited a computer expert from the community to speak to the class even though he was not a robotics expert, and a student interested in the foreign service asked a professor of political science to come speak.

Activity 3

Students research their chosen careers using sources such as the *Occupational Outlook Handbook* and *The Encyclopedia of Careers and Vocational Guidance*. Students are required to research the job description, education/training required, entry-level salary and salary range, job opportunities and outlook, and job location. They also research the cost of college or training. *The College Cost Book* is a good source for this information.

Activity 4

Using the information gathered in research, the students write pamphlets about their careers. Computers and word processing programs are available for typing the pamphlets. The pamphlets must be illustrated either with student artwork or computer graphics. The students spend several days editing and cutting and pasting their brochures for teacher approval before making the final copies. Careful planning is essential to the production of a professional-looking finished brochure. We photocopy the rough copies on construction paper or tag board for the final copies.

Activity 5

The final activity is the most exciting for the students. Each professional that the students invited to class comes to speak. We schedule two a day so each speaker is allowed about 20 minutes. The students prepare questions for each speaker and each student is responsible for introducing his or her guest.

The greatest value of having the speakers lies in what they tell the students about the importance of being able to think through problems, to solve problems that do not have apparent answers, and to communicate with others. The speakers stress the fact that the problems they encounter in everyday life do not have answers that are in a book somewhere. Another important piece of information the speakers share with the students is the fact that it is just as important to be happy in one's work and to feel that one is making a contribution to the world as it is to earn an acceptable salary. Most students realize that a prestigious job and a high salary do not necessarily guarantee happiness and a feeling of self-worth, but it is important that they hear this from someone whom they consider successful.

The career unit is one that we have refined in small ways each time that we present it, but we feel that it is a unit that is valuable one for the students. Most of our speakers have said they wished they had been afforded the opportunity to explore different careers while they were in school.

Karen Renner is the counselor serving students at Friona Elementary School in Friona, Texas (79035).

Works Cited

Clendening, C. P., and Davies, R. A. (1980) *Creating programs for the gifted*. New York: Bowker.

Hirt, S. J. (1990) "The importance of career education." *Challenge, 8(4),* 17-20.

Student Bibliography

The College Cost Book. (1991). New York: College Entrance Examination Board.

Cutler, Arthur. *Job & Career Planning 1985-1995.* (1985) Meadow Vista, CA: CFKR Career Materials, Inc.

Hopke, William E., *The Encyclopedia of Careers and Vocational Guidance.* (1990). Chicago: Doubleday & Co.

Occupational Outlook Handbook. (1985). Washington, D.C.: U.S. Department of Labor, Bulletin #2205.

Chapter 2
Math and Science

"Star Struck"—An Activity
For Young Astronomers
Techniques For Helping Students Understand
Astronomical Concepts Through Creative Projects

By Tom Weldon

Contrary to some opinions, astronomy is an interdisciplinary study. Literature contains many astronomical references and astronomers use the tools of mathematics to track the movement of planets. Throughout history, humans have conducted a kind of "astronomy"—giving names to individual stars and to groups of stars that appear to cluster together. Different cultures have offered various names for these imaginary pictures in the sky.

These pictures, seen by each culture that has shared this planet with us, can be used in an activity that touches several disciplines. Constellations, which are actually very useful maps of the sky, are fascinating to students at all levels. This activity on constellations, which will motivate and challenge gifted students, uses the constellations in a creative way and adapts, quickly and easily, to almost any grade level. This adaptation is made by modifying the complexity and depth of the information the students are required to present.

The activity need not be limited to science classes. It finds a home in social studies, reading, English, and math. It can be used to introduce such topics as celestial spheres, night observations, mythology, or even geography.

It is very important to understand, from the beginning, that the process students go through to complete this activity is of equal or greater importance than the products they develop. Investigative searches for information act as effective tools to help the students discover facts and incorporate them into their knowledge base. In order for students to derive maximum benefit from such searches, they must be given freedom of direction and considerable latitude to accomplish the assignment. The same concept applies to the development and use of the products for this activity (e.g., scripts, props, and costumes). Students should be allowed to independently select and develop their products. The teacher's role should be that of advisor and, when necessary, the source of some construction materials. If an evaluation for a grade is necessary, base the evaluation on a clear set of criteria which evaluate a product's creativity, the students' participation, and the accuracy of information presented. Grading only the correctness of facts, names, and astronomical information presented will be both unfair and counterproductive.

Those readers unfamiliar with the origin of constellation names and their importance to the modern astronomer might like to skip to the handout labeled "Star Struck" and read it before proceeding further. You do not need a strong background in astronomy in order to understand it. The handout should be passed out to students as a part of the lesson. It contains enough information to introduce them to the idea of constellations, their history, and their use.

Students should also have access to library facilities or a classroom resource center with materials related to the topics of astronomy, mythology, the mathematics of astronomy, and any other materials necessary. If using a library, students generally locate with ease all of the information they need from available reference sources. Most school and public libraries have a great deal of information on constellations. Ask students to begin their searches with encyclopedias, then lead them to explore books on the topic of astronomy and astrology. While the students are searching under astrology, it is important to discuss the difference between astronomy and astrology with them.

Procedure

Divide the class into groups of three to five. Cooperative groups, alphabetical groups, self-selected groups, or teacher-assigned groups seem to work equally well for this activity. The important thing is that there are enough individuals in each group to fill several roles. Although it will need to be repeated, inform the groups that during their class presentations, every member of each group must have an active role.

Read the "Star Struck" handout with the class. If possible, it should be reproduced for each group. Following delivery of the constellation information, present each group with a copy of the handout titled, "Star Struck Instruction." Be sure to fill in the blank in instruction five prior to duplicating the handout. This blank relates to the time students must use to present their presentations. The time limit you assign will depend on the grade level of your students and the time you have allowed for this activity.

Tom Weldon is the gifted education specialist and a science teacher at McCulloch Middle School (Highland Park, Texas 75205). He is a team member of the Project 2061 Science Curriculum Project and a past teacher in the Texas Governor's School. His forthcoming book, Creative Teaching Strategies for the Sciences *will be available in the Fall of 1993 from Prufrock Press (Waco, Texas)*

Student Instructions For "Star Struck"

1. From the list of 88 modern constellations, select one for presentation to the class. Although some of them have intriguing names, your group might consider selecting a more common one such as one of those in the zodiac. No two groups may have the same constellation.

2. Once your group has made its selection, write the name of the constellation and one alternate selection on a single sheet of paper and have each member of your team sign the paper. Then, submit the paper to the teacher. Constellations will then be assigned by the teacher.

3. Each group will prepare a presentation describing its constellation to the other groups. The presentation will not include any of the following: lecture, monologue, essay, or lettered chart. Possible alternatives are drama, mime, physical objects, games, or any other classroom-appropriate thing your group might devise. Purchased or public domain computer software will not be acceptable.

4. The presentation must convey the name of the constellation including the origin of the name and the myth or legend associated with it, and it must include the constellation's location in the sky including whether or not it can be seen from the school's geographic location (when and where). At least five major stars located in the constellation must be identified. Major stars include all named stars. If there are fewer than five named stars in the constellation, then the designation and magnitude of the five brightest stars in the constellation should be included in the presentation.

5. The minimum time for each presentation will be ____ minutes.

Creating Laboratories
Based On Student Interest
Strategies For Creating Multiple Laboratories
In The Science Classroom

By Maggie Rickard

As a biology teacher, my students frequently toss me the question, "Ahh, do we have to take notes again?" Somewhere, I think it was college, I got the brilliant idea that the only means of presenting factual information was to lecture in an increasingly dull voice to increasingly blank faces.

In an attempt to fight my students' boredom, I did use a few typical tools for the more comprehensive chapters of my text. For example, I pulled questions from the text which required one-word answers which could then be used to complete a crossword puzzle. The students, thrilled to be playing games in school, excelled at these activities as well as the subsequent tests. However, such strategies took my classes only so far. How was I to encourage my students to understand biology on a deep level with crossword puzzles and tests?

Fishing for ideas, I went back to my notes on reading and writing across the curriculum, where I found a favorite quote. According to Patricia Johnson, "What I have discovered is that writing helps my students understand science more fully than any other teaching strategy can" (1985). Combining that information with my own creative instincts, I came up with the following solution which worked well for me and my students.

The particular chapter I was struggling with covered mammals. After reading the chapter, the students were bursting with questions that the text did not answer. I decided to use those questions as a springboard for a rather lengthy, two-week research and writing project.

As my students shared their questions, I jotted them down. Then I asked each student to write down and turn in any questions they had which were not mentioned in the discussion. That evening, I narrowed the list to 25 questions.

During the next two days I went into action. My school librarian and I collected books and other materials which addressed, in a specific manner, the questions my students generated. I also gathered from my laboratory storage room preserved specimens which related to the students' questions. Finally, I called the representative at my regional educational service center and requested live specimens of some animals the students had asked about.

After collecting everything I needed, I organized several labs in my room—one lab for each question. For example, Susie, who frequently visits Sea World, asked about the differences between seals and sea lions. I brought in a book about marine mammals, turned it to a page which pictured the skeletons of both animals, and wrote a short paragraph about the diagrams.

Throughout this process, I documented the sources for my books and specimens. I did this to make sure setting up the lab during the next year would be easier.

Another approach to the task of creating the various laboratory stations involves assigning a question to each student and having students prepare the various stations. I suggest that this approach be taken after the students have been exposed to several teacher-created laboratory stations. This establishes for the students models for effective stations.

When class began the next day, I provided the students with a sheet of their questions, and we took a walk-around or exploration of the various stations.

The students, working independently, moved from station to station, studying diagrams, charts, preserved specimens, live specimens, etc. Their task was to answer each of the questions I had provided. Since most of the questions dealt with the differences between similar animals, many of the stations required comparison skills. However, since this lab was being used to whet the students' appetites for the main writing assignment, the stations provided only partial answers to the original questions, revealing only one difference between sets of animals.

After completing the lab, the students worked in pairs, selecting sets of similar but different mammals to compare. They were allowed to choose animals from the lab or other appropriate pairings. My original intention was to let only one student per class research each animal—no duplications. However, when one student, Sam, had his heart set on learning more about leopards (his favorite animal) and a group was already comparing leopards and lions, I decided to let Sam and his partner research leopards and tigers. That was probably one of my best decisions—Sam, a frequent discipline problem, became totally immersed in his work and presented me his finished paper with pride (he even typed it!).

Once the students had chosen their topics, we spent two days in the library reference section. I gave them suggestions for possible attributes to compare—physical traits, killing and eating habits, habitats, etc. I did not dictate the length of the paper—I only asked that they compare at least five attributes (Sam and his partner covered seven).

Each student researched one mammal and then compared information with his or her partner. When the students began the actual writing process, my only additional requirements were that the final copy be legible, written in complete sentences, and have all sources cited. Since many students learn from drawing, I encouraged graphs, maps, diagrams, etc.

The results of the drawings surprised some students. For example, when one pair wrote that leopards and lions lived in Asia, they visualized encounters between the two animals. After drawing and shading a map of Asia with red for lions and blue for leopards, they discovered that the two habitats rarely overlapped.

Another pair of students graphed the decline in population of their animals over the last years. They then asked me how to get in touch with wildlife preservation organizations. The drawings added a dimension to the students' knowledge that might not have arisen through words alone.

This project resulted in several positive results—more in-depth understanding of mammals in general, development of cooperative group skills, refinement of research and writing skills, and 100 percent participation. However, there were also some unexpected results, including the fact that some students developed an even greater appreciation of science, and everyone increased their knowledge of and respect for their environment.

Maggie Rickard is certified to teach both biology and English. She currently teaches at Kitty Hawk Junior High School (Judson, Texas 78148).

Works Cited

Johnson, P. (1985). *Roots in the sawdust: writing to learn across the disciplines*. Gere, A. (ed.). Urbana: NCTE.

Chapter 3
Humanities

First Person Presentations
Bring Historical Characters Into Your Classroom

By Tom Weldon

Almost all school curricula contain content that is essential but dull (or more precisely, DULL). Much of this content must be learned by students because it acts as a stepping stone on the way to deeper water within the discipline being studied. Fortunately, there are several teaching strategies that are highly effective in making such content both interesting and valuable for students. The first person presentation is one such strategy that I have used successfully over the years.

A first person presentation is a strategy in which the teacher assumes the persona of an actual person somehow related to content to be studied. The selected content is then recounted and taught from the persona's point of view.

As Old As Story Telling

First person presentations are similar to story telling, a strategy used by societies throughout the world to impart important cultural information from one generation to the next. In fact, both strategies share many of the same skills to convey understanding and promote retention. Of course, the greatest difference between the two is that in first person presentation, both the character portrayed and the story told are usually real.

This strategy works well for all levels, kindergarten through college, and in all disciplines. Students easily remember Pythagoras explaining the relationship between the sides of a triangle, Copernicus presenting the radical idea of a heliocentric solar system, Mark Twain reading some of his works, or Patrick Henry delivering his speech before the Virginia Convention (the famous "Give Me Liberty or Give Me Death" speech). The possibilities are endless. Even if the identity of a primary participant is unknown, a fictional period character (perhaps a newspaper reporter of the time) can be synthesized to relate the content.

A List Of Pointers

Of course, while the "actors" within our profession may find that this strategy comes quite naturally, the rest of us may need a few pointers to have a successful and fun attempt at a first person presentation. Below are ten tips to relieve your presentation anxiety and help you as you prepare a presentation.

1. Remember those times, when you were a child, when you put on some of your parent's or older sibling's clothing and played "dress-up." You are about to do the same except that now you are an adult—it will be even more fun, so plan to enjoy yourself.
2. Select the content your students will be learning. If this is your first attempt at a presentation, concentrate upon choosing content that is interesting to you and appropriate for your teaching assignment.
3. When choosing the character you will portray, identify a character who might know the content best or could provide a unique insight into the content. Don't always assume that this character is the first that comes to mind. For example, the portrayal of a close friend of the George Washington may be a better character choice then the stoic first president himself. At this point do not worry about details such as the costume or even the gender of the character you select to portray. As you become more experienced, you may want to use a fictional character to provide an unorthodox view of the content you are teaching. Beginners may find this latter technique too difficult because it requires a large amount of peripheral knowledge to create a convincing character.
4. Conduct a little background research into your character's life. You should know enough information about your character to present him or her in a realistic fashion. However, you need not spend hours in the library. Thirty minutes of research should be plenty of time for you to gather enough information to create your character. Your school's librarian should be able to point you to several reference books designed to provide efficient 3-5 page biographies of important characters in history. These books are perfect sources for the information you need.
5. As you study your character, try to determine the individual's social mannerisms and frame of mind as well as his or her physical characteristics. In addition, try to determine the mannerisms and customs of the time in which the character lived. It is the believable portrayal of the whole person that distinguishes a first person presentation from a lecture.
6. Developing the costume you will wear can be lots of fun. Beg, borrow, construct, or buy a few costume components that appear to be appropriate for the period. The theater arts teacher at your school

may be particularly helpful to this end. The costume you design need not be entirely accurate. Remember, it is the content you are teaching students not the details of a period's clothing—you are allowed to "fudge" a bit with your costume. Furthermore, there is no need for a complete wardrobe. Symbolic pieces are enough. Students are usually willing to suspend belief, and a simple statement of identity will suffice. However, a costume of some type is recommended as it reminds the performer to remain in character and adds a touch of the dramatic for students.

7.   A prepared script or expanded outline helps, although it is not essential for everyone. A script helps you focus your research, organize your presentation, deliver content more effectively, and help you manage your time. The novice may find that memorizing a few lines can improve peace of mind. However, do not feel rigidly bound to your script or outline. As in a classroom, each audience is different. If the performance is to appear realistic, you must be willing to react spontaneously with your students. Furthermore, feel free to break character when it is necessary—students will still be engaged with the presentation as long as you don't "loose" your character too often. If your character was a politician or orator, consider presenting a rendition of a famous speech by the character. Your school librarian will be able to point you to books containing such speeches.

8.   For your first performances, keep the presentation short—under twenty minutes. That amount of time will hold student's interest and reduce your stress. As you become more proficient, longer presentations will come naturally.

9.   Try not to include too many details or dates in your presentation. Concentrate on emphasizing the major ideas related to the content you are teaching. If you have difficulty identifying what is more important, ask yourself, "What things associated with this content do I or experts in this discipline remember and use." To help students identify key points from your presentation, prepare a handout of important questions that can be answered by listening and participating in the presentation.

10. Do not worry about encountering someone among your students who knows more about your character than you. Unfortunately, this rarely happens, but when it does, simply encourage the individual to become an active part of the presentation.

First person presentations work. They are fun for both teacher and student. After a few presentations, students will beg for more.

When that happens, encourage them to try it themselves. They will learn and retain an even greater amount by doing their own presentations.

Tom Weldon is a science teacher and gifted education specialist at McCulloch Middle School (Highland Park, Texas 75205). He is a team member of the Project 2061 Science Curriculum Project and a past teacher of the Texas Governor's School. He is the author of Creative Teaching Strategies for the Sciences *available in September of 1993 from Prufrock Press (Waco, Texas).*

'Till The Fat Lady Sings
Using Opera As An Organizer
To Build Integrated Units In History

By Michael Cannon

Currently, there is much interest in the teaching of units in the history classroom that integrate several disciplines within a single unit of study. An integrated study of a historical period ought to include an opportunity for students to integrate several subject areas such as art, music, and literature to ensure that students develop a more complete picture of a time in history. Such units of study can provide students with an opportunity to use a variety of research and study skills as they investigate a particular culture from many perspectives. However, an integrated approach to a historical period can become fragmented and lack focus. Unless care is taken, such units may become nothing more than a hodgepodge of "stuff" from a period in history.

Using Opera In History

I have discovered an effective technique for integrating several disciplines into my history classroom without loosing the integrity or focus of a unit. A representative work of art, either visual or musical, can help unify a unit of study. Opera, with its blend of literature, drama, and music, is well suited for this purpose. Opera adds another dimension to the study of history. It brings the atmosphere of the time alive in a way that history class alone cannot accomplish.

Although often dismissed as being uninteresting or too difficult for students, opera becomes more accessible when placed in its historical context. The right opera can serve as the nucleus around which a historical study revolves and as a springboard for creative expression. A study of nineteenth century Europe, for example, can be enriched and given new scope by using a videotape of Giacomo Puccini's *La Bohème*. Written in 1896 but set in Paris of the 1830s, *La Bohème* spans the nineteenth century and is particularly suitable for use in a historical study. Puccini based his opera on the novel *Scènes de la Vie de Bohème* by Henri Murger and is generally considered an accurate portrayal of artists and other residents of the Latin Quarter in the early decades of the nineteenth century.

Historical research can follow two related strands depending on the intent of the study and the needs of the students. Students can use the following worksheets together or independently. Handout One, "Paris in the 1800s," is focused on content and is broad in scope—covering politics, science, fashion, and cultural figures. Handout Two, "Cultural Background," focuses on the important people, movements, and ideas of literature, art, music, and philosophy of Europe in the 1800s. These areas reflect the vocations of four of the characters in *La Bohème*.

Time And Expectations

I suggest you communicate to students the degree of detail and depth of research you expect of them on the worksheets. Depending on the amount of detail and depth of research you require, your students may need one or two weeks to complete the worksheets. While encyclopedias contain the basic cultural background information, specialized reference books are helpful. The cultural background study may be enhanced by assigning students to read books by the authors listed on the "Cultural Background" worksheet. While students conduct their research and prepare their projects and presentations as described on the worksheets, the teacher can begin to familiarize the class with the opera. A recording of highlights of this opera is an excellent introduction, whether the teacher has specific musical objectives in mind or just wants students to be familiar with the music before viewing the opera.

To help students see the value of music in telling a story, ask them if they prefer television or movies with or without music. Elicit from them examples of how music is used to further action and cue emotions in the audience. As they listen to the recording, help them identify the different voice types of the characters: soprano (Mimi), mezzo soprano (Musetta), tenor (Rudolfo), baritone (Marcello and Schaunard), and bass (Colline). Ask the students to explain how the characters might be different if their voices were different, if Rodolfo had a bass voice or Mimi had a low contralto.

An easily recognized musical device is Puccini's use of the reprise (repetition of the melody). Have students or groups compete to identify reprises heard during the tape. Another technique to listen for is music illustrating the details of action on stage. The first act contains several examples including the burning of Rodolfo's manuscript and Colline tumbling down the stairs.

Background Information

Information about *La Bohème* is available from many reference sources, but two of the best available works are *The New Kobbe's Complete Opera Book*, and *The New Milton Cross' Complete Stories of the Great Operas*.

Both of these books contain plot summaries and notes on the music. Another useful reference is the spring 1990 issue of *Arts Scope*. This publication of the Metropolitan Opera Guild contains some of the activities listed below as well as the summary reproduced in Handout Three.

After reading the synopsis of *La-Bohème*, discuss "bohemians," using dictionary definitions as well as the student's own ideas. Ask students to name modern bohemians.

To focus students' attention during the video, assign students to one of the main characters: Mimi, Rodolfo, Marcello, and Musetta. Have each of the four groups take notes on the character, including the character's physical description, personality, and motivation. The students' task is to become an expert on their assigned character—to be able to describe that character to others.

While watching the opera, be prepared to stop the video at any point and introduce characters or explain what is going on. The opera runs about two hours, so you may want to divide the viewing time into two or three days.

The end of Act II is a good place to break the viewing. Take time to discuss the characters and the events after each act or as it seems appropriate. You can make watching *La Bohème* special by having an opera party complete with "champagne" (sparkling grape juice) and "French pastries" (cookies).

After watching the opera, class discussion is very important. To help generate discussion of the characters, have the students assigned to each character meet, pool their notes, and develop a group profile of the character. Then, divide the class into different groups of four with a student assigned to each character in each group. The group members, as experts on their character, share their insights with the rest of the group.

The discussion of characters can lead to, or be a preparation for, a discussion of the interrelationships between the characters. Have students identify the conflicts between each of the major pairs of characters and relate the conflict to modern drama or to events in their own lives.

The following are suggested final projects for *La Bohème.*

1.   You have been selected to design the set for a brand new production of *La Bohème.* Choose an area in your town that represents a contemporary setting for Act II. Use a familiar café, restaurant, or tavern in this area as a focal point for the scene, and create a set design. Include a descriptive paragraph for your set.

2.   You are the librettist (script writer) for *La Bohème* and Puccini wants you to rewrite the ending of the opera. Change the ending so that one of the artists becomes successful and wealthy. On the basis of what you know about the character, how does his/her success affect the other characters in the story? Use dialogue to rewrite the ending.

3.   You are the costume designer of *La Bohème.* Draw costumes for each of the four main characters (Mimi, Rodolfo, Marcello, and Musetta) as they would look in the 1830s and then as they would look in modern times.

La Bohème is not the only opera that makes a good focus for a historical period. *Tosco* (Italy during the Napoleonic invasion), *Aida* (ancient Egypt), and *Madame Butterfly* (U.S. intervention in Japan in the 19th century) are just a few possibilities.

Michael Cannon is a history teacher and gifted and talented program assistant for El Paso ISD (El Paso, Texas 79925).

Works Cited

"La Bohème," (1990, September) *Arts Scope.* New York: Metropolitan Opera Guild.

Cross, M. (1967). *The new Milton Cross' complete stories of the great operas.* Garden City: Doubleday & Company.

Harewood, G. (1969). *The new Kobbe's complete opera book.* New York: G. P. Putnam's Sons.

Handout One
Paris In The 1800s

Politics

1. Who was the ruler of France during the 1830s? How did he come to power?

2. Describe the main political events of the early 1800s.

3. What were the relations between France and its neighboring countries?

Fashion

Describe the usual forms of clothing for both men and women in the 1830s. Be sure to include men's and women's hats.

Science and Trade

1. What were the usual forms of transportation at this time?

2. What would have been some of the most common businesses and professions?

3. Name famous scientists of the time. Tell what each discovered or invented.

4. Name one important medical advance of the nineteenth century. Name at least two diseases fatal at the time but curable now.

Cultural Figures

1. Name three writers who were active during the 1830s.

2. Name three composers who were active or were still popular at this time.

3. Find the names of at least three French artists painting during the nineteenth century.

4. Name an influential philosopher of the time.

Handout Two
Cultural Background: The 1800s

Choose one of the following areas. With your assigned group, look up the people and concepts listed and prepare a five to ten minute presentation for the class. Be prepared to present examples of representative works by these artists, writers, composers, and philosophers.

Literature

Important People
Honorè de Balzac, Victor Hugo, Alfred Lord Tennyson, Stendahl, Johann von Goethe, Robert Browning, Charles Dickens, Edgar Allen Poe, and Alexander Pushkin.
Concepts
Romanticism, the Gothic novel
Note
Prepare a poster about the authors and read aloud from the works of at least three of the writers.

Art

Important People
Camille Corot, Eugène Delacroix, Jacques Louis David, Jean Ingres, Honorè Daumier, Edouard Manet, and Edgar Degas.
Concepts
Neo-classicism, Impressionism, "art for its own sake"
Note
Prepare a poster or other visual aid and use art reproductions from books, slides, and prints to show examples of the works of these artists.

Music

Important People
Ludwig von Beethoven, Frederick Chopin, Franz Schubert, Giacomo Puccini, and Richard Wagner
Concepts
Romanticism, opera
Note
Prepare a poster of one or more composer(s). Locate recordings of their compositions and play a section of each piece for the class.

Philosophy

Important People
Georg Hegel, Immanuel Kant, Jean Jacques Rousseau, and Arthur Schopenhaur
Concepts
Noble savage, dialectical logic
Note
Make a poster with illustrations and quotations from these philosophers.

Handout Three
The Story Of *La Bohème*

Characters

Reproduced
from "La Bohéme"
in *Arts Scope*
(Spring, 1990)

Opera in four acts
by Giacomo Puccini;
Libretto
by Giuseppe Giascosa
& Luigi Illica;
after the novel
by Henri Murger

Mimi (mee–mee): seamstress (soprano)
Rodolfo (roh–dol–foh): poet (tenor)
Marcello (mahr–chel–oh): painter (baritone)
Musetta (moo–zet–ah): shop girl (soprano)
Schaunard (shoh–nahr): musician (baritone)
Colline (co–lee–neh): philosopher (bass)
Alcindoro (al–seen–doh–roh): councilor of state (bass)
Benoit (ben–oy): landlord (bass)

Setting

Paris, Latin Quarter, 1830-1831

Act I
In The Attic

On Christmas Eve, the painter Marcello and the poet Rodolfo are working in their tiny attic high above the rooftops of Paris. They try to keep warm by burning the pages from Rodolfo's latest manuscript. Colline, a philosopher, joins them. Their other roommate Schaunard, a musician, arrives with food, money, and firewood.

While the four young men enjoy the unexpected abundance of food, their landlord comes for rent. They get him tipsy, pretend to be shocked by his latest romances, and send him away without his money. They divide Schaunard's money and head for the Café Momus. Rodolfo, who has stayed behind to work, answers a knock on the door. He meets Mimi, a pretty neighbor whose candle has accidentally gone out. Rodolfo relights her candle, and she prepares to leave but discovers she has lost her key. While they look for it, both candles in the room blow out. Rodolfo takes Mimi's frail, cold hand and tells her his hopes and dreams; she replies with the story of her life as a seamstress. It is love at first sight, and, arm in arm, they join Rodolfo's friends at the café.

Act II
Café Momus

The streets are bustling with holiday crowds. Rodolfo buys Mimi a bonnet before introducing her to his friends. Marcello's former girlfriend, Musetta, enters the café on the arm of a wealthy older man named Alcindoro. Singing a bold waltz about her popularity while trying to attract Marcello's attention, Musetta pretends her shoe pinches and sends Alcindoro off to get her a new pair. As soon as he leaves, she embraces Marcello. After a military band passes, she departs with the bohemians as Alcindoro, back with the shoes, is presented with the bill for all their meals.

Act III
At The Gates Of Paris

At dawn several months later, Mimi walks through the snowy outskirts of Paris in search of Marcello. She tells him about Rodolfo's constant jealousy and his intention to leave her. Hiding in the shadows when Rodolfo steps from the nearby inn, she overhears him confess to Marcello that his real reason for separating from Mimi is because of her frail health that can only worsen in their poverty. Mimi stumbles forward weeping and coughing and bids a tender farewell; however, they decide to stay together until spring. Musetta and Marcello, in contrast, part from each other angrily trading insults.

ACT IV
In The Attic

Spring arrives, and Rodolfo and Marcello lament their separation from their sweethearts. After Colline and Schaunard bring them a skimpy meal, Musetta urgently enters and says Mimi is below, too weak to climb the stairs. She has come to die near Rodolfo. While Mimi is made comfortable, Marcello goes to sell Musetta's earrings for medicine, and Mimi and Rodolfo are left alone tenderly recalling their first meeting. After the others return, Mimi dies. When Rodolfo realizes what has happened, he runs to her side desperately calling her name.

Educational Theater: More Than Show Biz
Educational Theater Should Be An Exciting Component Of THe Language Arts And English Classroom

By Annabelle Howard

Editors Note: Annabelle Howard, a classroom teacher of many years, is the author of Classroom Classics, *a program designed to bring to students an understanding of a culture, its history, people, and art, through the use of drama. The materials she developed so intrigued me that I asked Ms. Howard to write the following article offering an introduction to the use of drama in the classroom.*

It is unfortunate that most theater activity in the schools is relegated to the "extra-curricular." No other activity is as capable of combining so many curricular concerns and of benefiting students of all ability levels and all styles of learning as theater. Even the study of dramatic literature *as literature* is hampered by a suspicion that theater is somehow too much fun to be educational and by a reluctance felt by teachers who have little or no experience with theater to undertake theatrical productions.

The result is that school plays are most often staged in a way that mimics "show biz," musicals and other textually uninteresting plays cast through auditions that create a star system, with parents invited to a big opening night (often a fund-raiser), etc. At the same time, the plays that are studied in literature classes are studied on the page, not on the stage. Ironically, if schools were to stage the kind of plays that they want their students to study in literature class in a way that authentically reflected the way professional theater people stage those plays, the result would not be "show biz," but education of the most potent form.

Principles Supporting Educational Theater

Ten years ago, when I came to my realization of this dilemma, I began working on its solution. Let me enumerate some of the key truths upon which the kind of educational theater I prescribe is based.

Dramatic Literature Is Special

Gifted students particularly should be made aware that dramatic literature is radically different from prose fiction, poetry, or prose nonfiction. Shakespeare's work, tragically, is too often studied as poetry. Shakespeare was certainly a great poet, but his chosen literary form was that of the *play*. To understand a dramatic work, it is not enough to read a play from a textbook or from a paperback. Nor is it enough to see a live production of a play, and, certainly, it is not enough to watch a videotape. The dramatic form is never appreciated more deeply than by actors, directors, stage managers, and dramaturgs as they work from the blueprint of a script to create a theatrical event. It is the nature of a script that it is, indeed, a blueprint for action. The actual play is, as Hamlet might have said, another thing.

It is because a playwright shapes actions and crafts blueprints for theatrical productions that his or her professional title is play-*right,* not play-*write.* A playwright is a builder of sorts, and what he or she constructs is a dramatic *structure* made of hope and fear, confession and conniving. Aristotle was the first to formulate this truth succinctly: a play is an imitation of an *action*, while a poem, by contrast, is an imitation of a *thought.* Please keep this point in mind; I'll come back to it toward the end of this article. For now, it leads us to my next point.

Rehearsing A Play Is Not The Same As Directing Traffic

Too many school plays are rehearsed in the way one rehearses a graduation ceremony or a football play: The only thing at issue is where you move when. In the professional theater, much more goes on. The director's job is to construct a psychological "plot" of action and re-action, obstacle and adjustment, that maps the motivations of the characters through the drama. This is the same job performed by students of literature all the time, but this is *practical* literary criticism. To guide the actors' performances, the director must communicate his or her understanding of this underlying "plot" to the actors as they rehearse. Actors try to personalize this "plot" by thinking of when in their own lives they have had objectives similar to those of their characters. An actor must shape every word and gesture in a particular scene in such a way that it works toward his or her character's specific goal for that scene. Working on a play from the distant past, such as a Shakespeare test, the director and actors must come to understand the cultural assumptions underlying the characters' actions. How can we understand Macbeth's reaction to the witches unless we know that people in Elizabethan times were much more persuaded than we might now be about the power of witchcraft? As "modern" production may choose to re-interpret the text, but an *intelligent* modern production should understand the original context to make a meaningful choice to depart from it.

The Creation Of A World Is Always
An Education For The Creators

Set designers, costume makers, dramaturgs (theater professionals whose job it is, partly, to understand the theatrical and cultural
history of dramatic literature), musicians, choreographers, and stage
managers all work together to create the world of a play. In the case
of plays from the past, such as Shakespeare's plays, this involves a
study of the art, the music, the dress, the architecture, the food, the
etiquette—the world of Shakespeare's time. It is impossible to achieve
this act of creation without learning a great deal along the way, and
learning it not only through language but also through sound, sight,
and movement. In short, all possible learning styles, all possible "intel-
ligences," are engaged in the act of making theater.

No One Can Think For You, Learn For You,
Or Act For You

Students of all ability levels benefit enormously, and improve
enormously, the moment they take responsibility for their own learning. When a student has a role in a theatrical production, whether it is
to act the title role or to paint the backdrop, his or her responsibility
is clear and tangible. It is my experience that students of all ability
levels accept this kind of tangible responsibility much more quickly
and enthusiastically than they might the more abstract responsibility
of performing well on tests, research projects, etc. A related benefit of
theatrical production that is especially applicable to gifted students
is the genuine open-endedness of the process. There really is no one
right answer, and it is important to pose truly open-ended challenges
to gifted students who are often lulled by the ease with which they can
get the right answer in less open-ended activities.

Bring Drama To Students

Now, let me take you back ten years when, in a K-12 school in
Washington Heights in New York City, I taught 5th grade "homeroom"
subjects and 3rd grade French. The history textbook began with a bor-
ing chapter on the Greeks, and I decided to do something different. I
searched all over New York City's great libraries and universities for
a version of an ancient Greek tragedy translated and adapted into
language my students could manage. I wanted them to experience the
concerns and conflicts that would have been meaningful to Greeks of

the period. When I found no such version of a Greek play, I wrote an adaptation of the Greek play with which I was most familiar: *Antigone*.

The project garnered more intense and sustained interest than I could have expected. Students virtually would not allow me to teach any lesson that wasn't in the service of rehearsing the play. In response, I devised lessons that took some aspect of the play as a touchstone to explore a language arts or social studies topic in my curriculum.

To make a long story short, I then adapted *Macbeth*, Molière's *The Bourgeois Gentleman,* Pedro Calderón de la Barca's *Life is a Dream,* and many other plays, committing to paper the techniques I had developed. After several artist-in-the-schools residencies, foundation grants, and teacher-training institutes, I began self-publishing my materials. Teachers in all fifty states ordered my materials and in many cases urged and guided me to expand and redefine them. Recently, Sundance Publishers & Distributors acquired my materials and now publish them under the series name Classroom Classics.

Practical Guidelines

There are a few important practical principles that have guided my work and should be helpful to any teacher interested in using theater in the classroom. These practical principles should be of use to teachers in any exploration of the educational use of theater.

First, find a play that will work for your classroom, that has educational content, and preferably, one that is brief enough to be read aloud in one school period. Students are best introduced to a play whole, so that the complete arch of the dramatic action is apparent. If you do have theater experience, you may like to do improvisations with your students. These are valuable but only in their proper place in the process. Improvisations are valuable when students are trying to use their own experience to better understand situations in the play, but improvisations are not a replacement for a text from which the students can learn something. In general, improvisations reaffirm things students already believe rather than getting them to explore things they do not already know.

Second, permit students to provide the impetus to produce the play. Remember that the mission is education not "show biz." The first oral reading will have to be a teacher-driven, in-class assignment. But, even if you plan to produce the play, let it be the students who make the commitment to the enterprise. In the discussion after the first reading, ask leading questions like "Would this be a play that you'd like to put on in this class?"

Third, if you decide to produce the play, do so minimally. Students may make costumes if they like, but use every opportunity to promote learning rather than stage fever. For example, perform educational plays in your classroom, not in the auditorium. Tie the play to other literature that is thematically or historically connected. Phrase such extension assignments in a way that builds upon the students' interest in the play. For example: "If you'd like to better understand why somebody would behave like [a character in the play], you should read [a book that features a character who behave similarly or faces a similar problem]." Other extension activities are possible; in fact, if the play is an important one from an interesting period, the possibilities are virtually endless.

When you get past the first reading, you don't have to cast your best students in the lead roles. If the school year is well under way and you know your students well, you may find many more interesting reasons for casting students in particular roles. A student who would find the theme of a play particularly compelling, even if he or she struggles academically, might be motivated to make the stretch to perform a lead role and benefit beyond measure from the experience.

An interesting piece of trivia that I encountered in researching the Greek theater continues to give me encouragement. In Athens in the fifth century B.C., it was a civic duty for Greek citizens to perform as a member of the chorus of a Greek play. The plays were performed in annual festivals, and the rehearsals took a whole year. In rehearsals, young Greek citizens would study history (we know it as mythology), politics, literature, music, and dance; an understanding of all of these was considered essential to a good performance. In fact, being a part of the chorus served as the formal education of a young Greek citizen. Given the many legacies of fifth century Athens—philosophy, logic, aesthetics, democracy—it is encouraging to know that the idea of using theater to teach also dates from that important historical moment.

Annabelle Howard, a teacher of many years, is the author of Classroom Classics. *Information about her works may be obtained from Forrest Stone, Managing Editor, Sundance Publishers & Distributors, Newton Road, Littleton, Massachusetts 01460. Ms. Howard may be contacted through her publisher.*

An Apology To Socrates
Effective Strategies For
The Language Arts Classroom

By Lisa Stogner

"**O**kay, folks. Settle down. Socrates, close the window and take a seat. Yes, I know it's a beautiful day." Daydreaming again. How did that kid ever get in my gifted class?

"We've got about fifteen minutes left before the bell rings, and I want to discuss tonight's homework. If you are industrious, you can get started in class. Stop groaning. Yes, it's an essay." Why do they always gripe about writing assignments? After all, I am giving them a chance to express their opinions!

"The topic is on the board. I'm sorry, Socrates, that you don't like the topic. No, I choose the topics." How dare he challenge me! Who does he think he is? I'll never forget the day he tried to interpret Thoreau!

"Now, with Socrates' permission ... I want a five paragraph, 500-word theme, written in third person. No, five paragraphs ... count my fingers, Socrates. What? When you become a famous writer, you can then write in first person. Until then, stick to third." Ha, famous writer! He can't think, much less write!

"Any other questions? If not, get busy." Finally I can sit down and grade those three-week-old papers ... too much to do tonight ... gotta read *Animal Farm* before I teach it tomorrow ... where's my red pen?

"Socrates, what are you gabbing about now? Honestly, you are a glutton for conversation. The topic? This is not a group project! If you and Plato don't shut up, I'm moving you. Well, I'm sorry that you have writer's block. Perhaps if you sit quietly, an idea will hit you." Where's my red pen? Found it! Let's see ... well, ee, you still haven't mastered capitalization and punctuation ... F for you.

"What now, Socrates? If I helped you, this would be my paper, not yours, right? Okay, so you know nothing and that's all you know. Think, Socrates, think! I don't want another cave essay. Dark, light, chains ... that was weird stuff. I want deep, philosophical writing, got it? Now, go back to your desk and write." What's this kid's problem? Maybe I need to recommend him for counseling. Records show he's the brightest kid in the class, but I don't see it. He had better learn how to play the game, or he will wind up in prison someday.

"That's the bell, folks. See you tomorrow." Thank God; they're gone. If these kids are the leaders of the future, we're doomed. Where's my red pen? ...

A Realistic Scenario?

Is this scenario realistic or exaggerated? Are you shocked and disgusted with the student, teacher, or both? Would you like to discover some new research that may enhance your teaching and make you and your students happier and more productive? If so, answer the questions below with either true or false.

_____   1. Daydreaming and talking are not acceptable forms of prewriting.
_____   2. Writer's block is due to a lack of creativity and intelligence.
_____   3. Students, for the most part, do not like to write.
_____   4. Teachers should always dictate the writing form.
_____   5. Students favor reflexive (personal) writing rather than extensive (expository) writing.
_____   6. Teacher-student conferences are valuable if the teacher is not the critic.
_____   7. Red pens should be used when evaluating student papers.
_____   8. Teachers do not perceive students as writers.
_____   9. The teacher in the scenario understands and utilizes the writing process.
_____ 10. The teacher in the scenario owes Socrates an apology.

Discoveries And Explanations

Question 1: False

Have you ever been deep in thought, seemingly unaware of your surroundings? Were you "goofing off" or were you thinking? Writers "percolate" just like coffee pots; they must brew awhile before the product emerges (Romano, 1987). In addition, have you ever needed to talk through a problem with a friend? Sometimes we just need a sounding board, and then the "aha!" hits. Nancie Atwell (1987), author of *In the Middle*, states, "Writing isn't just sitting quietly at a desk putting pen to paper ... writing involves talking. " Furthermore, are you the only one talking in your classroom? If you are not allowing students to discuss, debate, and share, then your "silent classroom is anathema to learning" (Emig, 1978).

Question 2: False

How many times have you been perplexed over that special project proposal grant or your classroom budget orders? Is this a form of writer's block? All of us, at one time or another, have found ourselves "stumped."

Does this mean we are stupid and uncreative? Once the seed has been planted, it must be nurtured (Murray,1978). The water, sun, and care he is referring to may be what the professional writers have called the "waiting" process. F. Scott Fitzgerald exclaimed, "To have something to say is a question of sleepless nights." If teachers recognize the "waiting" process as valid to young writers, they may be rewarded because we all know that "good things come to those who wait!" Can teachers shorten the "waiting" period? Yes; provide adequate time for prewriting (Murray, 1978) and keep in mind that you too have been "stumped" occasionally!

Question 3: True

"I hate to write" can really be translated as, "I am afraid to write." Students feel inadequate because "writing is unusually mysterious to most people" (Elbow, 1973). If the teacher is a writer and understands the writing process, this love will be the catalyst in the pinball machine. Students will "light up" and bells will ring! Another reason students detest writing is they believe no one "is interested in what they have to say" (Romano, 1987). Negative comments and "bloody" papers convince students we don't care about their opinions or feelings. It is our duty to lessen their fears and appreciate their voices.

Question 4: False

The clue to the answer is the word "always." Sometimes teachers must dictate the form of writing, but be careful that the form does not dictate the meaning! Granted, formulaic writing skills are necessary in today's "test happy" world; however, when the teacher seldom allows students to make their own choices, the teacher is stifling intellectual growth. Keep this in mind: "Successful learning is also engaged, committed, and personal learning" (Emig, 1978). Furthermore, how much attention should be paid to mechanical errors? Should a student fail because of one run or one fragment? Don't disregard errors, just put them in the proper perspective. What should be stressed is meaning and voice. Leave the mechanics for later (Romano, 1987). If the writing process is being stressed, errors will be fewer. One last thought to ponder ... several college students returning home to visit their teachers remarked, "Guess what? We can write in first person, and papers can be longer than 500 words!" These students were excited; Romano explains that "they've been cut loose."

Question 5: True

Don't you write best about what you know and understand? Writers prefer reflexive pieces. Perhaps teachers prefer extensive pieces because these are easier to evaluate; however, evaluating papers is so subjective regardless of the style. Reflexive papers lend themselves to sharing feelings, and emotions. "When we write, we reveal through language our thoughts and feelings" (Brufee, 1985). Do you want to tap the creative juices of your students? Sparks can fly if reflexive prompts are given. Wouldn't Benjamin Bloom be proud to see us moving past the analysis stage to the synthesis level? Isn't it ironic that teachers traditionally assign extensive essays, yet the classical literature studied in the English classroom is reflexive in nature? Students will have a greater understanding of universal truths if we allow them to discover their own truths. They will discover "mucho" similarities, and isn't that what we hope to accomplish?

Question 6: True

True, but so hard to do! When conferencing with students, it is often difficult to keep your mouth shut. Conferencing is imperative because we have the need to share what we've written; we have the need to share our ideas with the "writing expert," the teacher. But ... beware expert, you don't want the writer to feel belittled. Lucy Calkins (1986) reminds us, "Don't be the critic ... be a person." Guide the student by asking thoughtful questions; concentrate on content, not mechanics. Don't write on their papers! After all, it is not your paper, is it? Celebrate with the writer and be thankful for the sharing. You don't want your students to leave the conference dejected; but instead, energized, wanting to write.

Question 7: False

Is your red pen a cherished member of your family? As English teachers, we are notorious for "bleeding" on papers because we earnestly believe we are not doing a good job if the ink doesn't spill. Actually, we are doing more harm than good. If you must mark, use a pencil and write in the margins. You might try a new technique; try writing comments on a separate piece of paper and attach it to the essay (Romano, 1987). Consider giving up the red pen; you may discover encouraged, unafraid young authors who are willing, even eager, to write.

Question 8: True

Authors write, students write. What's the difference? We don't perceive our students as authors, do we? We bleed on their papers, we write critical comments, and then we slap on a grade. "We don't assist students by observing what works and doesn't work with them" (Calkins, 1986). Writing should be so profuse in a classroom that it becomes second nature, then writing will become powerful (Romano, 1987). If writing becomes powerful, voice is found, the "gate is opened," opinions matter, and perceptions change. Students will see themselves as authors if their ideas are published; the teacher can't be the only audience. Who knows what could happen? After all, didn't someone teach Shakespeare?

Question 9: False

The evidence is clear; this teacher does not understand or utilize the writing process. Prewriting did not occur other than fifteen minutes of class time. There was no prompt, no sharing, no reading/writing connection, and no thinking. The paper is a "due tomorrow" product. Will the students predraft, revise, or edit? It's doubtful. Will they publish? Again, doubtful. The teacher in the scenario is using "the dominant method of composition instruction that has existed since the late 19th century" (Calkins, 1986). The teacher needs help, do you agree?

Question 10: True

Socrates is already in prison—this classroom! He and others like him, are being taught to hate English more than they already do. Sad, isn't it? No wonder Socrates gave his ideas to Plato who wrote them down, so eloquently in dialogue form ... something Plato must have learned from some other teacher. He did manage to survive. How? Who knows? But not all are so lucky.

I'm sorry, Socrates.

Lisa Stogner has her master's degree in gifted education from the University of Houston. She has taught for eleven years and is currently teaching English at El Campo High School, El Campo, Texas 77437.

Works Cited

Atwell, N. (1987). *In the middle*. Portsmouth: Boynton/Cook.

Brufee, K. (1985). *A short course in writing*. Boston: Little, Brown, and Company.

Calkins, L. (1986). *The art of teaching writing*. Portsmouth: Heinemann.

Elbow, P. (1973). *Writing without teachers*. New York: Oxford University Press.

Emig, J. (1978). "Writing as a mode of learning." *College Composition and Communication*.

Murray, D. (1978). "Write before writing." *College Composition and Communication*.

Romano, T. (1987). *Clearing the way*. Portsmouth: Heinemann.

Mythology and Culture
Making Connections With
Past And Modern Cultures
By Michael Cannon

The stories found in classical mythology provide a vast resource for teachers. While the tales are fascinating in their own right, they also provide a means for investigating the beliefs and values of the culture that produced them. In reading these stories, students gain insight into cultural universals and can then produce their own contributions to mythic evolution. The following activities may be used with a study of classical mythology, the Middle Ages, or creative writing.

Part 1
The Classical Myth

The myth of Orpheus and Eurydice may be used to illustrate how a myth reflects the values of a culture. The myth of Orpheus and Eurydice can be briefly told. Orpheus is a singer of amazing power, charming not only every person who hears, but the trees and rocks as well. He marries the beautiful Eurydice, but his happiness is destroyed when she is bitten by a snake and dies. Refusing to accept the separation of death, Orpheus goes to the Underworld and uses his singing to obtain her release from Hades and Persephone. The only condition is that while the two leave, Orpheus cannot look back at Eurydice until they reach the upper world. At the last minute Orpheus forgets the warning and turns to see if she is following, and loses her forever. A complete telling of the myth may be found in Robert Graves' *The Greek Myths* (1957).

After discussing the story with students, group them into small groups and direct them to write a one or two sentence summary of the story. Write the summaries on the board and after a discussion of each, erase all but the one the class chooses as the best summary.

At this point you may want to introduce the concept of literary archetypes. The idea of archetypes was introduced by the psychologist C.G. Jung, who defined them as the "basic forms and pathways in which our psychic existence is enacted ... and [which] have been elevated to the ranks of deities and heroes" (1959). In literature, these are symbols, story patterns, or character types that recur frequently and evoke strong, often unconscious, associations in the reader. Archetypal characters include the young hero, the wicked witch, the wise old man, the endangered princess, the fatal woman, a trickster, one that falls from grace, and various threatening monsters. Settings are often a dark forest, an enchanted island, the land of the dead, or the wasteland. The story patterns flow from the characters, with journeys, rescues, and descents into the land of the dead as common events.

Use the summary of the myth of Orpheus on the board and discuss with students the archetypes of the hero, the endangered maiden, and the journey into the land of the dead.

Now ask the students to go back to their small groups and list what they think the morals or themes of the myth are. Write the group responses on the board, noting which ones are repeated. Have the class rank the top three or four themes with the greatest accuracy or summary power. These may include the triumph of love over death, the power of music, and the inescapablility of fate. Include these yourself if necessary. Ask the students what the themes reveal about the beliefs of the people who told the stories. This could be a discussion, debate, or the basis for an essay.

Part 2
Medieval Transformations

The story of Orpheus was also popular with the Romans, and Ovid included it in his *Metamorphosis*. It was through Ovid's work that the story of Orpheus and many other Greek myths were transmitted to the Middle Ages. Medieval scholars even adapted the tales of Ovid to make them more consistent with Christian teachings. The myth of Orpheus underwent an amazing change, being transformed into a marvelous new creation, "Sir Orfeo." The tale was written in Middle English in 1325, about fifty years before Chaucer's *Canterbury Tales*. It combines the myth of Orpheus with Celtic magic to produce a fairy tale with a happy ending. The original text is in Garbaty's *Medieval English Literature* (1984). A modern English version of "Sir Orfeo" may be found in Loomis and Hibbard's *Medieval Romances* (1957).

By comparing this version of Orpheus to the original, the students can identify the changes in character, theme, and plot and then explain what these changes reveal about medieval society and culture. The summary in the adjoining side bar may be used if the complete version is unavailable.

After reading "Sir Orfeo," have students (individually or in groups) compare this tale with the original myth, listing the differences in both of the stories and those elements which have remained the same. List the differences on the board and have the class rank them in order of importance in terms of the insights they provide into Medieval culture.

Sir Orfeo

Sir Orfeo was a great and generous King of England, son of King Pluto and Juno, those gods of days gone by. Courteous and brave though he was, Sir Orfeo was also renowned as the greatest harpist ever heard. His wife was Queen Heurodis and he loved her with all his heart.

While sleeping beneath a tree one day, the queen had a frightening dream. She dreamed that a mysterious man came and demanded that she go with him to his land. She refused and he warned her that he would return for her the next day. The king was so concerned about the dream that he ordered that she be guarded by 1000 knights on the following afternoon. In spite of all his precautions, Queen Heurodis simply disappeared from the middle of all the guards.

Sir Orfeo was so distraught that he left his kingdom in the care of his steward and went to live as a hermit in the wild forest. Dressed in rags and animal skins, the only reminder of his former life was his harp. The wild animals were the only audience for his music.

Some 10 years later, Sir Orfeo saw his lost queen riding in the company of a troop of beautiful women. He recognized them as women of Faerie, and he secretly followed them into their land. It was a beautiful country with a royal castle in the middle of a broad plain.

Sir Orfeo followed them into the castle and in the courtyard he saw a gruesome scene. There lay his wife, Heurodis, asleep, surrounded by other mortals who had died. They were all in the state in which they had died, some being burned to death, others drowned or strangled. Posing as a simple minstrel, he asked to play before the ruler, who was none other than the King of Faerie.

Sir Orfeo's playing so overcame the king that he promised to grant whatever wish the harpist might desire. Sir Orfeo promptly asked for the freedom of Heurodis. After some hesitation, the king agreed and restored Heurodis to Sir Orfeo.

Sir Orfeo and Queen Heurodis left the magical realm and returned quickly to their own kingdom. After first testing the loyalty of his retainers, Sir Orfeo resumed his throne. He and Queen Heurodis lived long and ruled the kingdom with wisdom and justice.

Use this ranked list of differences as the basis of a discussion of what might be inferred about medieval culture and values as reflected in "Sir Orfeo." This may be developed into an essay.

Part 3
Orpheus In The Modern World

The Orpheus myth provides a wonderful basis for creative writing. First, have students list on the board the essential characters and plot structure that are common to both the classical myth and the medieval version. The plot may be quite complex or no more than a musician's wife dying and his attempts to rescue her from the Underworld and its king by means of his music.

Students use these elements as the framework for their own writing. Just as "Sir Orfeo" reflected the medieval world in which it was told, their own stories should reflect contemporary values and concerns. Their Orpheus may be a popular musician, actor, or other charismatic figure. The Underworld could be the underworld of drugs and crime. Discuss the possibilities with the class, eliciting as many responses as possible. Encourage them to write something truly original, using the myth as the initial inspiration but going beyond to something new.

After the student's stories have been written, edited, and shared with the class, you may want to make a class book with the original myth, "Sir Orfeo" and their own stories. Illustrations for each story can enhance the product.

Myths like that of Orpheus can by used to point out cultural values, illustrate archetypes, and as a starting point for creative writing. These activities will help students gain insight into their cultural heritage and realize that mythology has unlimited possibilities.

Michael Cannon has taught students for eighteen years. He currently teaches humanities at Bassett Middle School, El Paso, Texas 79930.

Works Cited

Garbaty, T. (1984). *Medieval English Literature.* (ed.). Lexington, Mass: Heath.

Grave, R. (1957). *The Greek Myths.* Vol. I. New York: Braziller.

Jung, C. (1959). *Basic Writings of C.G. Jung.* New York: Modern Library.

Loomis, R. and Hibbard, L. (1957). *Medieval Romances.* (ed.). New York: Random House.

Classroom Dinner Theaters
Bringing Play Writing And
Production To The Classroom
By Sheila Gann

Crazy? What was I thinking? After attending numerous gifted and talented workshops which criticized the errors that teachers make by assigning gifted students work that is not differentiated but only more of the same, I decided to challenge my 1990-1991 English I Honors students' creative abilities more than I had the previous year. Echoing in my mind were effective gifted program principles:

- Build upon the characteristics of the intellectually gifted.
- Evaluate success within the program on the quality of the work produced by students rather than by tests of mastery of lower level skills (Fox, 1986).

Another factor that began to influence me pertained to the ideas of well-known theorists. Several prominent theorists of gifted and talented education, including Sidney Parnes and Joseph Renzulli, address and stress the importance of directing products toward real audiences (Maker 188, 216). With those things in mind, especially my responsibility to the students, I decided to implement some new strategies into my teaching.

After we read, discussed, and tested content from several one-act plays and *Romeo and Juliet*, instead of measuring the students' knowledge of drama and theme development by an exam, I challenged them to write and perform a one-act play which would be presented as a part of a dinner theater.

At first, the students were not receptive to the idea. Then, the more discussion the class members had about the viable possibilities, the more excited they grew. As their excitement and anticipation mounted, the creative ideas began to flow like a fountain. As rationale for my sake, I remembered the areas that could be addressed by going beyond standard achievement requirements:

- making judgments according to criteria;
- using resources;
- discussing and debating;
- taking part in class meetings involving group process;
- planning future activities; and
- evaluating experiences (Barbe & Renzulli, 1975).

The criteria that Barbe and Renzulli outlined for gifted projects seemed to pertain to the dinner theater that we were planning.

Suddenly, the magnitude of the dinner theater and all it involved struck me. I had gone into the project without any knowledge of directing, acting, play writing, raising funds, delegating chores, or hosting a dinner—to name a few. Realizing what I had created and begun, I shared my idea with our junior high school Sixth Grade Enrichment English teacher, Jeanette Stafford. She enthusiastically agreed to participate and include her class as well. As the students worked on the play, Jeanette and I worked on the administrative aspects. The parents began to offer their assistance. I immediately delegated the fund-raising task to one of the parents who offered to help. She contacted parents from Jeanette's class and my class. Many of the parents were eager to donate time and money. We set up a system so that parents who donated money would receive tickets to the dinner theater or discounts on tickets, depending on the amount donated. Jeanette found a caterer. At this time, we also scheduled a banquet hall. The parents and students sold tickets for $5.00 which included the meal and entertainment. All together, we sold and/or distributed 180 tickets for the dinner theater.

Meanwhile, the students had decided that they wanted to do a one-act play of vignettes about high school life. We used class time to sign up for writing, acting, and backstage teams. During these beginning stages, we continued with additional subject matter in the classroom. Other administrative tasks were taken care of at this stage as well. I developed a contract of responsibility for the students to sign, announced grading criteria based on participation and contribution, and set various deadlines.

Finally, the writing team had a rough script. It had decided to have vignettes of parent/child interaction, classroom scenes, gossip, and friendship. The writing team and I worked on the script to develop cohesiveness and theme. The one-act play focused on teen-age pressures caused by school, parents, friends, and relationships.

Once the class and I had developed a complete script, we realized that the performance would only take about thirty minutes because of the briefness of the play; therefore we invited Jeanette's class to provide an introduction and conclusion, or framing, for our production. The framing linked sixth-grade students to ninth-grade students, thereby illustrating the universal problems and concerns that all students have.

Because of the enormous amount of time involved in such a production, I set up a binding rehearsal schedule. Three weeks before the production, (up until now, we had spent about two months of thinking, planning, arranging, and writing) the students had to recite their lines to me; two weeks before the production, the acting groups (students involved in the same scenes) had to practice seven times a week in my classroom in addition to class time rehearsals. During this time, we abandoned additional class work and used the time to rehearse.

The night before the performance, we met in the banquet hall for the first time. Because of donations from the parents, we had excess money, so we catered sandwiches for the kids. After four hours of stressful, productive (at times) practice, we decided to call it a night.

The final hour came, April 27, 1991, 6:30 p.m. The cleverly designed programs created by my students were ready; the caterer had arrived; the decorations were in place; and the students had anxiously arrived. A complete bundle of nerves, I made my opening speech of greetings and gratitude before Jeanette's class served the guests at their tables. Finally, the moment that we had all anticipated came. The students performed flawlessly. My cameo appearance (the kids made me perform, since they had to perform) even went off without too many flaws. The audience gave us a standing ovation—what exhilaration. The overjoyed parents and community asked about subsequent performances and praised the students. Not only had the students used and focused on various learning processes to produce a product, the parents and community came to respect the creativity, intelligence, and dedication needed in such a massive project.

Crazy? What was I thinking? Well, it turns out that I probably was a little crazy for starting something about which I knew nothing. I plunged into the project without a detailed plan or direction. But, I learned a great deal about myself as a teacher and as a person. I discovered that it's okay to go on impulse and take chances; consequently, the students begin to play a role in directing instruction and creating new ideas. All gained from the experience, my students, the parents, the community, and me. An indescribable closeness that I never thought possible flourished between the students and me, and he experience enhances my confidence about teaching. I took a chance and it paid off!

After wandering aimlessly through the dinner theater project, I began to develop a checklist so that I could refer to it during future adventures.

Tips

1. Get permission from the principal and find an available date on the school calendar.

2. Turn the kids loose. They will come up with ideas.
3. Find money through fund raising, donations, or school funds.
4. Develop a contract of responsibility with the students that states that their grade is dependent upon their active participation.
5. Decide on and articulate the grading criteria.
6. Elicit participation from parents.
7. Team up with other teachers if they show an interest.
8. Book a banquet hall or find a place on campus that would suffice for dining and entertaining.
9. Find a caterer or parents interested in preparing the meal.
10. Allow students to sign up for writing, acting, helping backstage, and making decorations.
11. Set deadlines for rough and final scripts.
12. Set up a rehearsal schedule.
13. Decide upon decorations, props, costumes, and a price range.
14. Borrow props, decorations, and costumes from the drama department.
15. Develop a program to be handed to the audience which credits all persons who participated, including those people who donated money, time, or other items.
16. Conduct dress rehearsals.
17. Have students arrive early on the performance night so that they can eat prior to the arrival of the audience.
18. Recognize all persons who were instrumental in the dinner theater process on the night of the production.
19. Pat yourself on the back for attempting and following through with such an enormous production.

Sheila Gann teaches English at Edna High School in Victoria, Texas 77904. Her students often speak of the positive experience this unit provided them.

Works Cited

Barbe, Walter B. and Joseph S. Renzulli, eds. (1975) *Psychology and education of the gifted.* New York: Irvington Publisher.

Fox, Deborah. (1986). *Teaching english to the gifted student.* Eric Clearinghouse on Reading and Communication Skills Series. (October 30). Eric ED 270 782.

Maker, C. June. (1982). *Teaching models in education of the gifted.* Austin: Pro-ed, Inc.

World Explorations:
A Humanities Program

By Fran McMillan & Sandra Morris

W orld Experience is a humanities program for gifted sophomores at Newman Smith High School in Carrollton, Texas. It
is a two-hour block class that combines world history, world
literature, comparative world religion/philosophy, and art/music history with a "hands on" approach to learning. One teacher is history certified; one is English certified; but both have humanities backgrounds
and continue to take courses to strengthen the humanities core of the
curriculum.

World Experience is the follow-up program to the American Experience
program for gifted ninth graders. The eleventh and twelfth grade gifted
programs at Newman Smith do not continue with the humanities block
but concentrate on advanced placement history and English programs.
World Experience provides sophomores with a rare opportunity to experience a high level, cross-curricular approach to history, English, and related
humanities, always with a concentration on developing the writing and
thinking skills of the tenth grade gifted student.

Student outcome for World Experience combines the essential
skills and knowledge for world history and tenth grade English as
well as special gifted outcomes identified as appropriate for learning
enrichment.

One unique aspect of the World Experience program is its organization. Since our district divides its grading cycles into six six-week
periods, we found it helpful to divide our curriculum into six thematic
units—one for each six-week period. We use world history as the skel-
eton upon which to build our humanities study.

Six Thematic Units

- **Unit 1:** **Ancient Civilizations**—The Roots of Humanity:
  Our Key to Originality
- **Unit 2:** **Classical Civilizations**—Suffer Into Truth: The
  Classical Quest for Meaning
- **Unit 3:** **Medieval and Renaissance World**—Midnight or
  Dawn? The Struggle of Good and Evil
- **Unit 4:** **Age of Exploration and Discovery**—Breaking Into
  the Beyond: The Search for Land and Knowledge

- **Unit 5:** **Age of Revolution**—Pressing Against Authority's Wall: The Birth of the Common Man
- **Unit 6:** **Modernity**—War and Peace: Coming of Age in a Paradoxical Century

Developing Units

For each unit, we center our study on a historical time period and an accompanying theme. For example, our Unit 1 theme, "Roots of Humanity: Our Key to Origin-ality," focuses on the concept of human origin. In this unit we study pre-history, ancient Egypt, Mesopotamia, India, and China.

We plan our lessons in three-week cycles. During the first three weeks of a six-week grading period, we offer students an accelerated curriculum. Using lecture, seminar discussion, response-discussion to film, as well as parallel cooperative learning and role-play, students are moved rapidly through a large amount of content. During this three-week cycle, the teachers are responsible for students learning the general historical chronology of major people, places and events and for reading samples of the great literature of the period. Also during this accelerated portion of each unit, we present the development of music and art along with the philosophical and religious mind-set of the age.

After administering two objective exams at the end of the three-week period, one for history and one for literature, we move on to the next phase of the unit cycle where the students build on their knowledge-level foundation by learning to create something completely new and relevant for themselves. The reason that we compact so much learning into the first three weeks of the unit is to allow students a chance to explore and experiment with their own interests and talents for the final three weeks.

During the latter three weeks, we involve students in two activities that allow them to apply their learning in various ways. The first activity, completed during week four of the unit, is the intuitive essay. The second and culminating activity of the unit, completed during weeks five and six, is the "I-Search."

The Intuitive Essay

Since the academic emphasis of our class stresses the humanity of man's family, we foster that collaborative spirit in composition. At the conclusion of the three-week accelerated cycle and after the objective test over the unit, each student uses a full week (ten class hours) to compose a process paper that synthesizes the history, literature, art, music, and philosophy of the period.

Each student is encouraged to develop an original insight about what we have studied. For instance, a student might choose to base a paper on a metaphor like the flame in the pre-history film, *Quest for Fire*, thus tying all the ideas together with the extended metaphor of the flame of communication that spreads from the beginning of time through the ancient river valleys.

We suggest that students first devise a planning chart where they find specific examples of the metaphor/idea from history, English, and enrichment activities. Using the chart, the students then free-write their ideas into multi-paragraph expository essays and read them aloud to small editing groups which offer suggestions on organization, structure, and additional detail. After making editing changes to refine style and grammar, the students have access to a computer-equipped writing laboratory where they can use word processors and grammar and spelling checkers to design and refine their final copy before turning it in.

Students receive three test grades on their essays: one for historical content; one for style and literary application; and one for grammar (extra credit given for corrected grammar mistakes). Understandably, the first paper is the most challenging. We make copies of two of the best first essays, giving each student a copy to use as a model for future papers if needed. Once a student proves mastery of the expository original insight paper, the student may choose any writing style for later papers. This allows students who have mastered the writing form to try other creative approaches. One of our students has imagined a time-traveling dragon who flies into and out of each six-week unit time period. At the end of the year, the student will have a six-chapter novella that tours world history and literature.

The I-Search Project

Thanks to Roger Taylor's summer '91 workshop in out district, our I-Search project is a great success. We took Taylor's research project model, termed "I-Search," and molded it to fit our curriculum. His "I-Search" is a month-long project; ours is about two weeks so that it fits into our second teaching cycle in the unit.

The goal of I-Search is for each student to find out about some aspect of the particular historical and literary period, to research the facts, and to write a presentation that combines the research facts with some creative insight into the selected person, event, or movement. Some of the topics our students chose for this I-Search were: A comparison of Mid-East powers and strategies from ancient history to the Persian Gulf Crisis; burial rites from the Egyptians to the present; female queens from Hapshetsut to Catherine the Great; the Hittites; and a comparative view of Egyptian gods with later nature deities.

We take our classes to the library during week five. Students take approximately ten pages of notes from at least three sources. That week for homework, the students plan and organize their presentation. During week six of the grading period, our students have two class days (four hours) to refine their presentations. For the last three days, they share their findings with the class while displaying a visual product to illustrate their new learning—all in a ten to fifteen minute time frame.

Our students have produced some beautiful presentations. During the course of this school year, we witnessed a mummification, we partook of a Medieval Christmas feast, we viewed a short play about the persecution of the Christians, we heard a short story about an Indian girl's marriage dilemma, and we listened to a report about the present day King of Ghana and the history of his country.

It is obvious from the caliber of projects and products we receive from I-Search that the students not only learn the academics of history and literature, but they accomplish what all lovers of learning do ... they experience the relevance of their knowledge and see where they fit into the human family. We feel that there is no higher goal than to give our students a sense of "family," not only with the world through our study of academics, but also with each other.

The following is a typical weekly outline for each of our units:

- **Weeks 1-3:**   Accelerated approach to historical/literary material, with an emphasis on student retention (Objective tests over material covered).
- **Week 4:**   Students write intuitive essay, incorporating learning with personal insight.
- **Weeks 5-6:**   I-Search project preparation and presentation.

Field Trips

Our separate gifted budget in our district allows us to enrich the curriculum with one field trip every semester on the ninth and tenth grade levels and allows us to purchase some extra books, films, and other audio-visual aids. The first semester field trip this year, which occurred during the classical unit, included a visit to a Buddhist temple in Irving, Texas.

Afterwards, we viewed an Oriental exhibit at the Kimbell Museum in Fort Worth, Texas, as well as some works of Melissa Miller, a representational Texas artist who uses animal imagery in her vivid, large-scale paintings. Then we planned a stop at the Modern Art Museum of Fort Worth for the room-sized sculpture exhibit, *The Field*, followed by a meditative tour through the Japanese Botanical Gardens. In the past, we have attended Scarborough Fair in Waxahachie, Texas, and various Dallas, Texas, museums whose displays supplement our units.

Audio Visual/Film

Our enrichment also involves a direct teaching period in each unit. To teach music, we use a filmstrip/video kit, *History of Music (1-8)*, along with teacher-made hand-outs that guide note taking on the information. We also have a stereo system and CD player to produce background music from the time period, focusing on composers from the filmstrips.

Another book that helps us with the area of music history is *A History of Western Music* which we ordered along with the accompanying set of cassettes. For art enrichment, we use slides and movies from the PBS series *The Art of the Western World* and information from the book, *Timetables of History*. We also employ films to supplement the units.

In unit one, the students loved *Quest for Fire* along with short clips from the German film, *Wings of Desire*. For the medieval/renaissance unit, we compiled a series of clips to illustrate different facets of the period (*The Name of the Rose*, Errol Flynn's *Robin Hood*, *The Navigator*, and *Camelot*). During the classical unit, we viewed *Iphigenia*, a Greek film, as well as some clips from the Morgan Freeman *Oedipus at Colonus*.

Culture Project

The final enrichment plan, the Culture Project, focuses the students away from the school and into the world of experience. Once a semester, all students are required to visit a local museum or to attend a live theater performance or similar cultural event. Then they write a descriptive paper about the experience, making an analogical comparison to something else in their lives. Anytime, students may use additional culture projects as extra credit to boost low test grades.

Instead of a culture project during the second semester, we have student groups adopt a community service activity to perform. This project moves the students out of the classroom in an attempt to encourage them to share their energy and talent with the world.

Also, in addition to literature assigned and discussed in class, each student chooses one book per six weeks to read outside of class. At the beginning of the year, we give out lists of suggested novels from the past five years of AP English tests and other sources. We challenge the students to use this opportunity to get credit for reading something from the list that they have always wanted to read but never had the time for.

They create a 4x6 index card with a list of characters, a six to ten item summary, two to three striking quotes, and a personal rating. The card is turned in for a test grade.

During Unit Three when we read *The Tempest* together in class, each student chooses an additional Shakespearean play to read for the book card. Some of our students are voracious readers and can earn bonus points to boost low test scores by doing extra book cards. At the end of the year, each student has six or more cards. We encourage them to continue this practice so that when they take the AP English exam as seniors, they can easily review eighteen to twenty books.

Our World Experience program owns its success to many individuals. Because of the original vision of a secondary curriculum by Peggy Brown and Sylvia Butler ten years ago, administrative coordinators like Charles Blanton and Vicky Dearing, support from colleagues like Zoe Ellen Azzi, Tony Fracchia, Bert Hendrick, Jane Rice, and Barbara Taylor, the inspirational genius of Roger Taylor, and the encouragement of a nurturing school district, we have enjoyed the challenge of developing this stringent program which offers so many benefits to our gifted population.

Fran McMillan and Sandra Morris teach English, history, and humanities at Newman Smith High School in Carrollton, Texas (75006).

Writing For Other Audiences
One Motivating Technique For
Helping Students Develop As Writers

By Jamie Whitfield

Teaching students, even gifted ones, to write effective short stories can often turn into just one more task—for teachers as well as their students. My students used to listen to my lectures about plot resolution and character development. They then began writing and rewriting, hoping it would all soon be over. In the end, they were seldom satisfied with their results, wanting only to somehow please me enough for a good grade.

When grading their stories, I was seldom impressed with their soggy plots and their worn-out characters' actions and reactions. So, I would quickly move my classes to something new, searching for something that would light their intellectual fires, meet the curriculum requirements, and beat away that burned-out feeling so many teachers face. It seemed like an endless quest.

That is, until last school year.

Through a local writing project, I met Gay Gould, a second grade teacher at a school across town from the eighth graders I taught. Together we discussed the idea of linking older students and younger students in a pen pal network as a way to help motivate our students to write. At the conclusion of the conversation, we agreed to have our students exchange "a few letters." That conversation was a simple start to a wonderful writing experience for my students.

The experience began innocently enough with the arrival of a batch of second-grade letters. Gay's students drew pictures of themselves and wrote letters introducing themselves. Struggling with the phonetic spellings, tender egos, and limited written vocabulary shown in these second-grade letters, my eighth graders broke into groups of four to six and wrote letters back. We received photographs in the next batch and the information that they would be sending us something "special" for Halloween.

My students wrote back and then began to badger me about preparing something to send to the second graders in time for Halloween. I suggested each group send a "treat package," and while my students liked that idea, they wanted something more—something personal to send to these special pen pals who seemed to think of eighth graders as worldly, wise grown-ups. My students hit on the idea of creating an individual book for each special second grader. So, a new quest had begun.

The first concern was creating books which would be interesting to my students' young readers. My students began searching for ways to write for young children with limited reading vocabularies. A librarian suggested 15 young-reader books. My students analyzed these and determined that they all possessed the following characteristics:

1. The pictures, whether elaborate or simple, bright or pastel, were frequent and as important as the words.
2. There were picture pages with no words but never pages with words and no pictures.
3. The plots were designed to teach something useful in our society—honesty, familial loyalty, etc.
4. The characters were not always people, but often animals—sometimes with magical powers.
5. Words or phrases were often repeated to show emphasis and to teach new vocabulary.

With this knowledge, the students and I set to work. Our task was to have the books, a different one for each of the 28 second graders, ready in fewer than 20 days. I had only a few initial requirements: each group would do one book for a child, with a few volunteer groups doing two; groups would need to follow the time line I developed; each class would act as editors and quality control for those groups within that class; and I would try to find access to a comb book-binding machine so that the books would look "published."

The students agreed to my requirements and began work with the following guidelines:

1. Decide who will do what. (Who will draw the pictures? Who will write the words? If more than one plot suggestion is made or if there are any disagreements, how will the group decide what will happen?) This was to be written down, checked by the group for content and mechanics, and submitted to me by the end of the second day.
2. Decide on a basic plot line. (Some groups decided to mimic one of the popular books we had studied, but many groups decided to develop their plot around something personal about their particular pen pals such as moving to a new school, wanting to be principal, or being afraid to swim.) This plot line was also written, edited, and submitted to me.
3. Design a front and back cover for the book. (These had to be cre-

ated early to allow time for our librarian to laminate them.) The books could be any size or shape, but I suggested the covers would look more "professional" with construction paper. Some groups created their covers on typing paper and glued that to the construction paper; others drew directly on the construction paper.

4.   Complete a rough draft of the book, with written plot and artwork. (This allowed the students to decide where to put artwork or where artwork was needed.) These were given as group presentations to the class and allowed students, not me, to find many inconsistencies such as a character who fell and scraped a knee on one page and was miraculously healed by the next page.

5.   Create the final copy of the book; present it to the class; then, submit it to me. I found a company willing to let me use its binding machine to bind the 28 books. Any group missing this deadline would not have its book bound (every group was on time).

Once all the books were bound, I displayed them in the room. On the day their books were put on display, the students brought in the "treat bags" for their pen pals.

The treats and books were scheduled to go to the second graders the next day, the day before Halloween. Some groups went overboard with their treats. Other groups, afraid their pen pals would feel slighted, asked me to hold the books and treats until the next day so they could bring in more goodies.

Since we would still be able to deliver our surprises on time, I agreed, and separated the books and bags that were complete from those that were not. The books and bags that were ready to deliver were placed in paper sacks on the floor beside my desk, and the others were put back in the cupboard.

That night it rained.

Then, our roof sprang a leak.

When I opened my door the next day, the last day before Halloween, my floors were flooded, the bags of treats were soaked, and many of the books were ruined.

I stood in the middle of this huge puddle and cried. I went to the faculty lounge to call maintenance and cried. And when I had to face the students to tell them that their work had been destroyed, I cried. I knew that some of the second graders would not receive their books and bags, and I had no solution.

But a remarkable thing happened. The groups whose books had been damaged began to see the problems and to discover their own solutions.

The books were destroyed, but they were sure they could remake them in fewer than 7 hours. They wrote out letters to their other teachers explaining the situation and got permission to stay in the room all day. The artwork could be redone, the words rewritten.

The artist of one group was absent. That group went to the science teacher for a heat lamp and heat dried every page of its book.

Students discovered that if they held the pages up to the window, the artwork could be traced in less time than it would take to redraw.

The soggy stuffed toy that one group brought in to accompany its story about a dog was taken to the home economics room and tossed in the dryer.

The librarian agreed to do a rush job on the covers. The only problem was rebinding the books. Barnett Securities, the company that had originally allowed me to use its machine after hours would be in the middle of a busy day. I called and explained the situation. They told me to bring the books in any time! I took them over and bound them at the end of our school day and then rushed to deliver then across town to Gay.

The next day, 28 second graders received books and treat bags from my students. They were told of our disaster, but not which books had been damaged and redone.

Although they never learned who had the last minute books, they did learn some important lessons from my students. Gay told me later that one of her second graders was amazed that my students went to all that trouble because he thought "big kids aren't supposed to like little kids."

Across town my students were treated to the second graders' project—a huge Halloween mural. The mural contained Halloween images of ghosts, goblins, witches, and monsters created by the second graders. Many of the children included stories with their pictures. My students rushed to the mural when they saw it to find the work of "their" pen pal.

That night I reflected on the experience. Not only had my students mastered all of those writing skills and high-level thinking skills I had tried so hard to instill by teaching story writing, but they loved doing it. They just needed an audience. Also, they used their problem solving abilities to meet a real challenge as a group, and isn't that the way we usually solve problems in the "real world"?

Jamie Whitfield teaches English and journalism at Southside Middle School (Jacksonville, Florida 32216). She also coordinates the communications component of the magnet program in her district.

Words, Words, Words ...
Teaching Etymology To Students Can Be Informative And Surprisingly Fun

By Coston Frederick, Ph.D.

Many words have remarkable stories behind them. Beyond the denotations and connotations of words we spend so much time on in school, many words have stories behind them—sometimes marvelous stories. Tracking down those stories is a linguistic science called *etymology*.

But why bother gifted students with etymology? Very simple: "Reading is an intellectual and deeply personal learning experience, determined primarily by the reader's background of experience and need to know" (Frederick, 1984). The more teachers can tap into their students' backgrounds and their curiosity, the more intellectual stimulation and personal involvement in learning will occur. And, besides that, it is fun! Almost 400 years ago, Francis Bacon wrote, "Studies serve for delight, for ornament, and for ability." Bacon's statement is still true; otherwise, why bother with learning? Let's try a few words, especially for delight and ornament.

Paraphernalia

No, this isn't a lecture on drugs. It's too bad a perfectly good word has suffered from an association with such a negative concept. The etymology takes us back to the time when a prospective bride's father and the prospective groom haggled over what dowry the bride could bring to the marriage. Whatever it was—money, property, livestock—belonged to her husband after the wedding. After the groom and father settled on the dowry, they then forged another agreement, this time dealing with personal things the bride could bring to the marriage that remained *her* property, not her husband's. They agreed, you see, on *paraphernalia*. The word breaks down into *para*, meaning "beyond" and *pherne*, an old Greek word meaning "dowry."

Clue

Not many people would bother to look up this word in a dictionary. After all, we know the meaning. Some have even played the game. But the etymology of the word is perhaps even more interesting than the present meaning. If you look up the word in a good dictionary, you will not find many surprises in the definitions. But you may find "clew," which tells the etymologist—even amateur ones—to check out that spelling. It's British, and it comes from a Greek word meaning "a ball of yarn." A ball of yarn? Yes. Do you remember the story of Theseus on the island of Crete when he entered the labyrinth to slay the Minotaur? Other men had tried it, but they got lost in the labyrinth and perished. Theseus' friend Icarus (who later died trying to fly) suggested that he take a ball of yarn with him and unravel it on his way in. After he debated life or death with the Minotaur (Theseus won the debate), he then *followed his clue* out of the labyrinth.

Man

Here's a three-letter word that no one would ever look up in a dictionary. But it has an interesting story. A good dictionary lists about 20 definitions and uses of the word.

Try this one: Zoology—a member of the genus Homo, family Hominidae, order Primates, class Mammalia, characterized by erect posture and an opposable thumb (*The American Heritage Dictionary of the English Language*, 1976).

Wouldn't that be fun to memorize? (Ugh!) But wait! Opposable thumb? What's that all about? Scientists tell us we are the only species whose thumb can be used opposite the fingers. Other primates use their thumbs like another finger. Then, we investigate just a mite further in the dictionary and discover that, originally, *man* meant *hand*! Just for fun, let's look at some common words that contain *man* and have, or had, something to do with *hand*.

- manacles—handcuffs
- manicure—care of the hand
- manipulate—control by skilled use of the hands (this one has changed over the years)
- manual—labor by hand; also, a keyboard
- manufacture—hand made (changed after the industrial revolution)
- manure—to spread by hand (really!)
- manuscript—write by hand (clearly, before printing presses and typewriters)

Bedlam

Many people know this word comes from the name of an insane asylum centuries ago in Great Britain. The inmates were chained to walls and treated as animals. One story relates that townspeople would pay a fee and watch the inmates being fed, much like in a zoo. You can imagine the noise and odors that came out of a place like that! No wonder bedlam means uproar, noise, confusion. Sort of like your homeroom, sometimes.

However, not many people know that the original name of the "hospital" referred to was Saint Mary of Bethlehem, and *bedlam* is the British shortened form of *Bethlehem*. Pretty much like Worcestershire sauce pronounced "woostasheer."

Maudlin

Here is another word that went through a British word reducing salon. We know maudlin now as something overly sentimental—a real tear jerker—such as a maudlin movie, or a maudlin story. Actually, the word is a shortened form of *Magdalene*, referring to Mary Magdalene, specifically, that incident where she showed a great amount of emotion toward Jesus.

Many more words in our language have interesting etymologies. For example, you might track down the word *humor*, which will lead you to the words *sanguine, phlegmatic, choleric*, and *melancholy*—all descriptions of moods or personal dispositions. Also, you might find out why *dungaree, denim* and *jeans* all refer to the same material. Where did those words come from?

There are two basic ways etymology can be approached in class. One is simply to identify several words from reference books that lend themselves to etymological interest and introduce them to a class. Then the class can be given several to track down.

However, the follow-up is probably more important, to keep the students involved in etymology. This is best handled in *all* academic subjects—science, social studies, literature, etc. All words that are important to the content are subject to etymological analysis. Not all words will provide an illuminating history, but many will.

The most effective strategy for getting students interested in etymology is to do it as naturally as possible. Most teachers will not have to look for esoteric words for interesting stories. Note that the words described above are all quite common.

The first strategic step is for the teacher to do his or her homework and identify the words to be learned by students. These may be words identified in the content being taught or may be words in which students have shown an interest.

The second step is for the teacher or a group of students to do some initial detective work in order to see if any of the words have interesting etymologies. Some teachers and student groups have been pleased to find words they have been using for years have unusual stories behind them.

The third strategy is to use the student's background experiences and their curiosity to "hook" them into finding the stories behind a group of words. Such hooks might include questions such as those found below.

- "When you get married, do you intend to take any paraphernalia with you?"
- "How could Theseus possibly help detectives solve a crime?"
- "What is a teacher really saying when she exclaims, 'This room is bedlam!'?"
- "Does the name Maud have anything to do with the word maudlin?"

One effective way to have students pursue the stories behind words is to have them work in groups of three or four to track down the story of a single word using the resources available to them in the library.

Once they have a story organized, the fun really begins. Their next task is to have each group teach the rest of the class the story behind their word. Some of the stories can be dramatized, some mimed, some dialogued, and some graphically presented.

All words have stories that reveal information beyond their definitions. Let students discover these word stories and have fun doing it.

Coston Frederick, Ph.D., has recently retired from his position as a professor of education at Boise State University.

Works Cited

Frederick, Coston. (1984). *Teaching Content Through Reading*. Charles C. Thomas, Publishers.
The American Heritage Dictionary of the English Language. (1976). Houghton Mifflin Company.

Studying Chaucer Through Physiognomy
A Study of Chaucer's Characters Can Lead Students To A Better Understanding Of Themselves

By Pat Watson & Johanna Wrinkle

"You never really understand a person ... until you climb into his skin and walk around." These words, spoken by Atticus Finch to his daughter in Harper Lee's *To Kill a Mockingbird*, reflect the basic desire to help students vicariously live with and learn through the characters in the literary selections we teach. The study of Chaucer's *The Canterbury Tales* addresses this need; Chaucer offers clues to the personalities of the pilgrims in his work by describing their physical appearances.

Chaucer is often one of the earliest authors students encounter in their senior year. His *The Canterbury Tales* lays an excellent foundation for novels to be studied during the senior year of high school. Chaucer introduces us to a group of pilgrims gathered in Tabard Inn in London—as varied and as interesting a collection of characters as one could hope to find anywhere. These pilgrims reflect a cross section of society in Medieval England.

To introduce Chaucer and his Tales, I first discuss with the students the highlights of Chaucer's life and why he chose a pilgrimage to reveal the life and times of the late 14th century. I explain that Chaucer used physiognomy as well as the humors to reveal the personalities of the pilgrims. I further explain that physiognomy is more than a person's facial and physical appearance. It is the relationship between a person's outward appearance and the person's personality and character (judging a person by his features). I use common and not so common examples as:

- red headed—quick tempered;
- fat—jolly;
- broad forehead—intelligence, breeding;
- very thin—stingy, bad tempered;
- red clothing—aggressive;
- black clothing—melancholy;
- blue—constant in love;
- green—lightness in love, envy;
- gapped teeth—bold, aggressive, traveler, amorous; and
- white neck—sign of licentiousness.

Physiognomy

I explain that according to medieval physiology people's personalities or temperaments are determined by the relative proportion of the humors of their bodies (choleric, melancholy, phlegmatic, and sanguine). I then go into specific examples of the humors and the personalities they influence that we will encounter in the "Prologue."

Sanguine

For sanguine, I use the example of the Franklin, who is described by Chaucer as "a sanguine man, high-colored, benign." The Franklin lived for pleasure and was an administrator of an estate. A ruddy-hued person is always considered sanguine. Sanguines are talkative, lively, promoters, vivacious, and congenial. After describing a sanguine to this extent, I ask if anyone feels that he or she is sanguine. Students have fun discussing who might be sanguine. To enliven the discussion, it works well to mention a teacher or principal who might have this type of personality. Next, I discuss the weakness of a sanguine. A sanguine's weaknesses are that he or she is nervy, changeable, overbearing, and interruptive. Discussing these weaknesses will produce lively comments.

Choleric

The second personality type is choleric. The Reeve "was old and choleric and thin." He never made a mistake, was a good manager, and accumulated money. The Squire and the Wife of Bath might also be choleric. At this point, I tell the students that we will read *Wuthering Heights* later in the year and that Catherine might be considered choleric; in addition, I point out that Eustacia in *The Return of the Native* is also choleric. Cholerics are confident, positive, self-reliant, inventive, and aggressive. Again, I ask students who they know who might be choleric. The weaknesses of cholerics are that they are gutsy, lofty, and tactless. This brings out the devious smiles of the students as they try to fit this personality to a person.

Melancholy

Chaucer seems to imply that the Doctor is melancholy. Chaucer says of him that "He knew, and whether dry, cold, moist, or hot./He knew their seat, their humor, and condition." A good example of melancholy is Hamlet; in fact, directors always have Hamlet wear black. Melancholies are pensive, analytical, profound, faithful, and orderly; weaknesses are depression, reticence, and resentfulness. Students might like to discuss public figures who appear to be melancholy.

Phlegmatic

The fourth personality type is phlegmatic. Chaucer's Oxford student or the Nun might be phlegmatic; in addition, if students read *A Tale of Two Cities,* they will find that Lucy is phlegmatic. Phlegmatics are serene, content, peaceful, and dry-humored. I mention some people who are phlegmatic; then I mention the weaknesses which are anxiousness, indecisiveness, and shyness.

For the more advanced students, a study of the humors can be further developed.

Chaucer believed that the four body humors (or moistures) were the source of disease and of personality types, much as we think of glands and genes today. Chaucer believed that the body fluids, or humors of which humans are composed—blood, phlegm, choler, and melancholy—with their "qualities" of hot, cold, dry, and moist, would determine character and behavior.

I use the following to show the relationship of humors and physiognomy:

Sanguine	blood	hot and moist
Choleric	yellow bile	hot and dry
Melancholy	black bile	cold and dry
Phlegmatic	phlegm	cold and moist

Personality Profile

After the discussion of personality types and the humors, we read the "Prologue," discussing the personalities (or temperaments) of the pilgrims.

After we read the "Prologue" and a couple of the tales, I like for the students to take a personality test. *Personality Profile* by Florence Littauer is an excellent one as she uses the same terminology used by Chaucer (Littauer, 1983). Another excellent test is the *Lahaye Temperament Analysis* which also uses the terminology that Chaucer uses (Lahaye, 1986). I have devised one that works well for me in the classroom (Wrinkle, 1992).

The fun of taking the personality test is that students can chart the results and start analyzing friends and parents. When I see and hear my students making such connections, I know that our study of Chaucer has been successful. By having the practical experience of taking a personality test, the students seem to remember the traits of the characters and are, therefore, able to apply this knowledge to all

the characters that they are introduced to in British literature the rest
of the year.

*Pat Watson and Johanna Wrinkle teach history and English in
Muleshoe, Texas (79347). They are the authors of* Tactics to Tackle
Thinking *(ESC Learning Systems, San Antonio, Texas). They are also
authors of several novel guides.*

Works Cited

Chaucer, Geoffrey. (1969). *The Canterbury Tales*. R. Lumiansky (tr.).
    New York: Washington Square Press.
Lahaye, T. (1986). *Transformed Temperaments*. Wheaton: Tyndale
    Housel
Lee, H. (1960). *To Kill a Mockingbird*. New York: Warner Books, Inc.
Littauer, F. (1983). *Personality Plus*. Old Tappan: Power Books.
Wrinkle, Johanna. (1992). *The Canterbury Tales Novel Guide*. Muleshoe:
    Watson & Wrinkle Publishing.

Chapter 4
Learning Across the Disciplines

Sandwich Seminars
Techniques For Bringing Local Experts
And Students Together Over Lunch

By Anne Cole

"**B**ring your lunch and a friend to hear a nurse of holistic philosophy speak on reflexology. Enjoy your lunch during her talk. Afterwards, she will demonstrate foot massage, in which you may participate with a partner. Bring a towel and wear jeans."

The above invitation was to one of the many Sandwich Seminars offered to gifted and talented students at Leander High School (Leander, Texas) over the last seven years. These lunch programs have exposed gifted students, their friends, teachers, and sometimes parents to a wide range of topics not covered in the conventional curriculum.

The seminars which feature guest speakers followed by a question-and-answer period promote exploration of personal interests and the opportunity for peer interaction.

Some Sandwich Seminars have included "Beyond War" with Barbara Carlson (a peace organizer); artificial intelligence computer software (software that thinks); bronze sculptor Jim Thomas; history writer James Haley; "Governor's School for Gifted Kids" with teacher Virginia Anderson; Carole Rylander speaking on party politics; Steve Ross from the University of Texas on sports information; foreign exchange programs; satire with John Kelso of the *Austin American-Statesman* newspaper; thinking with Robert Duke of the University of Texas; fashion photography with Miama Wong, formerly of *Vogue Magazine*; teen court with a municipal judge; Meridell Achievement Center for emotionally disturbed teens; and McDonald's Observatory.

Approximately 15 presentations take place throughout the year. We schedule them during the students' lunch periods. It is easier to schedule the speakers each six weeks since most speakers prefer to commit to a date in the near future than to a date that is six to eight months away. A two-month calendar is distributed to all interested students. Students and teachers attend these programs voluntarily. A teacher may even bring an entire class when the topic is relevant.

The size of the audience varies from a dozen to more than 100. Most of the presentations take place in the library (near the cafeteria), but the larger audiences meet in the lecture hall. To beef up a program given by an actuary on the topic of math careers, students were allowed to order out for pizza. That, along with the announcement of his annual salary, made the presentation one of our most successful.

Advance notification of coming programs is posted on the daily bulletin board in our school lobby, and personal invitations are delivered to gifted students during the school day. But, the programs are not exclusively for gifted students. Everyone is welcome.

Students are encouraged to suggest ideas and topics for potential programs. Networking is the key to finding speakers. Most speakers are agreeable and seem flattered when asked to speak. Contact with prospects is made by phone or in person followed by a letter which includes a time schedule and a map to the school. Someone meets the guest a few minutes early, introduces him or her to the principal, and sees that the speaker has a chance to freshen up before the presentation. The speaker is also provided a lunch, if desired. A thank you letter is written afterwards including news clippings and photos when available.

With the exception of two professionals who presented all-day programs, all the speakers have been provided at no cost to the school. Presenters are chosen from within the school and from the community.

Some teacher presentations have included the works of Tolkein, dream interpretation, philosophy, and music therapy. Sometimes students present programs from their own experiences such as a laser beam demonstration, travel slides, a Washington Summer Workshop, Boys' and Girls' State, and summer semesters at Harvard.

Former students have returned to give presentations on Oxford University, the use of HyperCard on the Apple Macintosh computer, drug abuse counseling, and acting in Hollywood. A few times one-on-one seminars have been arranged for students with special interests in such topics as flying an airplane, entering university life, organizing a service organization, or learning about the Air Force Academy.

Poet Grady Hillman and British actor Roger Jerome of England both have performed and lectured for all-day seminars. They were scheduled for morning and afternoon lectures with honors English classes. At noon, they performed several wonderful vignettes for Sandwich Seminars.

Two Sandwich Seminars on travel led to a European tour planned by gifted students during the summer of 1987. The first program, about a cruise on a luxury liner featuring nine meals a day, piqued everyone's interest. At the second program on European travel, the students learned they could see seven countries for the same price as the cruise. Since then, travel topics have become a tradition. Recently, students have enjoyed highlights of Europe and a slide-show "walking tour" of the London theater district.

These seminars end up being so much more than just a cursory overview of a country. During the course of these seminars, the students learn about each of the countries mentioned, currency, passport and visa requirements, special customs, and basic language necessities.

The seminars are an important component of our school's mentorship program. They allow students to sample some of the many opportunities available to them. Once they have been exposed to an opportunity, then our school's mentorship program can help establish a more formal experience for the students.

The seminars have led to several independent projects in the mentorship program at Leander High. Some projects have resulted in published books of poetry, portfolios of photography, an internship at the state capitol, a published cartoon, a modeling portfolio, art portfolios, and original music recorded at a sound studio.

The lunch program has shown the students are interested in knowledge for its own sake. The program has also enabled students, teachers, staff, and parents to see each other as learners.

The enrichment program would be easy to initiate at other schools regardless of grade level. The possibilities are unlimited.

Perhaps the most important outcome of the lunch program is the positive view it gives presenters and participants of the benefits and possibilities of public education.

Anne Cole, a teacher of over 30 years, currently teaches at Leander High School (Leander, Texas 78641). In addition to teaching English, she is in charge of the school's gifted and talented mentorship program.

Travel Europe From Your Classroom
Allowing Students To Explore Europe
Through Research And Journaling

By Cynthia Wilson

As a world history teacher, I have long thought that the most effective way to teach my course would be a world tour. Lectures on the Old Kingdom in the shadows of the pyramids, discussions about the Shang dynasty while cruising the Hwang Ho, and studies of the Incas after trekking to Macchu Pichu sometimes seem the only way to inflame the interest of my students!

But public school financing hasn't allowed the fulfillment of this dream, so I've come up with an alternative. The European Travel Log assignment gives students an opportunity to study other countries and their cultures from a perspective that differs from the routine lecture and textbook approach. It also creates a need for students to use many and varied resources for their research, and the students consistently maintain that it is "a whole lot more fun than a research paper." In addition to research skills, the travel log allows students to use their creative thinking skills.

The travel log assignment is divided into six sections with very simple and basic instructions. This assignment is open-ended and has very little structure, which allows gifted students to explore history in a multitude of ways. The first rule is that students must depart from and return to their homes. Secondly, each student must use at least fifteen modes of transportation during their travels. The students usually moan and say things like, "I'll never think of fifteen," but by the end of the class period after brainstorming various methods of travel, they're asking if they can use more! Students have been quite creative in this area, with typical travels including swimming or jet-skiing the English Channel, cross-country skiing through Switzerland and Austria, and para-sailing from Italy to Greece. One dreamer's tour started when his space shuttle flight failed and he bailed out over Spain.

The third requirement is that students must visit 21 western European countries, and I give them a list of those nations. Within each country, their only instructions are to "visit lots of historical places." Students are instructed to give a historical overview of each place they visit, basically answering the question, "Why is this place a significant historical site?" I do not give students a set number of places they must visit in each country. This causes a few problems because some students have trouble determining how many places make "enough."

I explain to these grade conscious students that the number of places they visit in each country is not a fixed number of points in their grade. As a basic rule of thumb, I tell them, "If you don't think you've visited enough places in a country, you haven't." Once they get involved in their research, they realize that their own interests determine where they go and what they see. Occasionally there are students who just do not want to do the assignment, and I must provide more specific guidelines for them. Otherwise, I would get log entries like, "I didn't care anything about seeing Belgium, so I just glanced out of the window as the plane flew over it." This situation has not occurred often in the 11 years I have been doing this, and the products are almost always full of information.

In addition to political units, I also have the students tour geographic sites. I have included rivers, mountains, lakes, plains, etc., that students must visit. This varies from year to year, depending upon the general interests of the students and my own whim. Usually I include nine or ten of these places.

Students are encouraged to include such travel tidbits as people they meet, food they eat, souvenirs they purchase, and even diseases they get. This has provided some wonderful and entertaining reading. Students have visited the sites of medieval villages obliterated by the Black Death and come away with bubonic plague. They have met heads of state, royalty, street people, spies, and criminals. They buy everything from beach towels and T-shirts to castles and islands. They sample local cuisine, describing what they eat and how it is prepared. They even complain of weight gain!

Students have very few constraints on them for this assignment. This is "Fantasy Island" time, and the instructions read:

"You will be happy to know that the only limits you have are those you place on yourself. This is important particularly in terms of money, but it also allows you freedom from the conventional notion that history is past. In other words, you may travel through time help build Stonehenge, paint caves in Spain, be part of the entourage at Runnymeade, and storm the Bastille!"

I admonish them not to alter the course of history, but offer them limitless possibilities for adventure! Very few students have chosen to travel through time, and even fewer have chosen to be poor travelers. They always have an abundant supply of money, whatever the currency, and that gives them even more opportunity to have fun with the assignment.

The format of the travel account is also up to the student. To get their minds going, I suggest travel journals, diaries, letters home, and articles for travel publications. I have had several students who taped their travels and turned in an audio cassette, and, while those were enjoyable, their length made grading them quite a burden. I have advised against that medium, but I have received some very clever products. In addition to my suggestions, students have created photo albums, sketch books, travel brochures and guides, and hand-made postcards.

For their research, students are advised to consult atlases, globes, travel guides and brochures, novels about travel, histories of Europe and European countries, encyclopedias, travel agents, people who have visited Europe, and anything else they can find. I require a bibliography with a minimum of seven sources, but I have rarely had a student use that few. Students are encouraged to use a wide variety of sources for this assignment, and information in places they have not considered before. They also learn methods of citing some odd or rare sources.

This is a very time-consuming assignment, so I make the assignment six weeks before it is due. Because it also takes a long time to grade the travel logs, I have students turn in their products the third week of a six-week period. So, the assignment is started in one six weeks and turned in the following six weeks. We spend three to five days in the school library getting started. By the end of that time, students are confident enough with the assignment that they need little further teacher assistance, and the rest of the work is done outside of class. Students report on their progress each week, and I occasionally remind them that this assignment demands minimal procrastination. Those students who wait until the last minute invariably do not finish, and their grades mirror their effort.

The travel log is an independent research project that is flexible enough to use in any history class. Gifted students are able to use their creativity and intelligence to take hold of a long-term project and follow it to its completion. The loose structure of the project lets the immediate rewards for the students come in the form of grades, which are consistently high on this assignment, and an increased awareness of Europe. However, their are some rewards that come later for my students. I cannot count the times that former students have grabbed hold of my arm and told me about their real trips to Europe. They tell me that they sometimes knew more about stops on their tours than their tour guides, and that they went to a particular place because they read about it when doing the travel log.

So, the assignment has some basic practical application as well. And, on top of that, it's a lot of fun!

Cynthia Wilson teaches honors world history at Jack Hays High School (Buda, Texas 78610).

World Class Travel Logs

The travel log assignment has provided much pleasure for me as I see the intricate and creative efforts of my students. There are many memorable travel logs in my past, but a few are exceptionally memorable. As a big fan of the Indiana Jones films, I was particularly amused when one of my students created the persona of Indiana's cousin, Carolina Smith, and went on an archaeological tour of Europe. As lively as any of the films, she had one death-defying experience after another.

Another of my favorites was actually a joint effort. One year, all the girls in the class decided they would meet each other at various time and places and do some sight-seeing together. The greatest event of the trip was Laura's wedding. Having met a prince and fallen in love, Laura was to wed. The other girls were her attendants, and wedding plans abounded in each log. Unbeknownst to the girls, the boys in the class decided they wanted in on the action. A few of them crashed the wedding!

A final favorite of mine was a monumental and creative effort in which a student wrote a travel account entitled "Garfield Does Europe." She made comic strips of Garfield eating and sleeping his way through the continent in his typical lethargic way. Hounded by Odie and frustrated by Jon, Garfield found his way through Europe and complained at every tour stop that didn't have a food stand. In full color, the travel log resembled a book of the Sunday funnies!

Gone But Not Forgotten
Using A Local Cemetery For A Valuable Learning Experience

By Myra Weatherly

Requiem

Under the wide and starry sky,
Dig the grave and let me lie.
Gladly did I live and gladly die.
    And I laid me down with a will.

This be the verse you grave for me:
Here he lies where he longed to be;
Home is the sailor, home from sea,
    And the hunter home from the hill.

—Robert Louis Stevens

Want to liven up your class? Head to the local cemetery. It's not likely this outdoor laboratory site will be crowded with tour groups or charge fees. However, a visit to a cemetery piques students' natural curiosity and provides valuable tools for studying local history, genealogy, math, geology, botany, and art. Hidden among the silent monuments of a cemetery is a wealth of information, waiting to be discovered.

A walk among the weathered stones of a cemetery is a useful resource in tracing the history of a community. Students become explorers as they learn which families were prominent in the community, individual and average life spans, how many children died in infancy, the military service of the community's people, and the diseases that caused death. Students also learn the meanings associated with symbols and epitaphs. In today's fast-paced and mobile society with its myriad of bewildering changes, cemeteries give students a sense of permanence and a link to the past.

This study is especially appropriate for gifted students in that it affords opportunities for using higher levels of cognitive and affective skills as well as providing for a variety of creative activities. It offers experiences in historical research, problem solving, and collecting, recording, classifying, and analyzing data.

Preparation

This unusual field trip requires planning. Search your community for a cemetery that is rich in history and worth exploring. Preview the cemetery to locate features that you want to emphasize. Scout out specific tombstones that will be interesting to your students. Know beforehand the trees and plants found in the cemetery.

Determine the types of stones used for markers. This varies, depending on the age and location of the cemetery. You are likely to find marble, sandstone, granite, slate, and various metals used most often. Acquaint students with these materials before the trip. It is a good idea to have rock samples in the classroom for the students to handle and observe. Memorial companies, especially those that cut their own stone, will be particularly helpful to this end.

Be sure to get permission for your visit from the person in charge of the cemetery. Inform parents of your plans and objectives for this unique field experience.

Invite someone who is familiar with the history of the cemetery and community to speak to your class before the excursion. If this is a cemetery connected with a church, this may be the priest or minister of the church. Otherwise, it might be someone from the local historical society.

If feasible, visit a gravestone rubbings exhibit at a museum. Museums exhibiting rubbings include the Freer Gallery and the Smithsonian in Washington, DC, the Metropolitan Museum of Art in New York City, and the Municipal Art Museums of Cleveland, Baltimore, and Seattle.

Literature sparks interest in a cemetery study. Have students read and discuss *Safe As the Grave* (Cooney, 1979), the story of twins whose curiosity about a Civil War era grave marker leads them to discover a long-lost treasure. Alternatively, have students read selections from Thomas Gray's *Elegy Written in a Country Churchyard* (1987).

Procedures

The following activities are designed to serve as a guide to a cemetery study and may be adapted and restructures to the representative student age levels and backgrounds.

1. Define terms relating to a cemetery study. The following terms may be used: epitaph, crypt, eulogies, mortician, cemetery, crema-

tion, boot hill, inscription, deceased, genealogy, symbolism, mortuary, catacombs, sepulcher, wake, requiem, shroud, funeral, corps, cryonics, mausoleum. Ask students to add to the list.

2. Discuss the meaning of symbols used on tombstones. Examples include ...
    - candle or hourglass—time passing
    - doves—promise
    - dove—innocence
    - feathers—the soul's flight to heaven
    - lamb—infant
    - skeleton or bones—everyone must die
    - sun—the soul will live forever
    - trumpets—victory
    - weeping willow tree—sadness

3. Introduce epitaphs. Point out that the earliest known epitaphs are those found in Egypt. The Greeks were master composers of epitaphs. Although many epitaphs are religious and philosophical, others are satirical and humorous. Ask your students to make a collection of famous epitaphs. Research humorous epitaphs. One good source for unusual epitaphs is *Best of Gravestone Humor* (Schaefer, 1990). Have students write epitaphs for historic figures they're currently studying.

4. Practice reading a tombstone. Make sure students understand how to use the dates of birth and death on a marker to determine the age at which the person died. Explain the meaning of only one date on a marker. Remind them to be aware of family names and family plots.

5. Brainstorm jobs related to a cemetery. Assign students to write help-wanted columns for a newspaper.

6. Investigate customs relating to burials. The following questions may be used: Are all corpses buried in the ground? Are some corpses buried above ground? Why? What is cremation? Is this practice more common in certain parts of the world? Where did the ancient Egyptians bury their dead? Why? Are bodies ever frozen? Why?

7. Have your students create a gravestone rubbing. Gravestone rubbing is a centuries old, relatively simple art that provides a

decorative momento of a visit to a cemetery. Rubbings were used in the Orient as early as the 7th century. Some of the best depictions of medieval life in Europe are the rubbings of church brasses in cathedrals.

Each student will need a sheet of newsprint or rice paper, masking tape, rubbing stick, and a wrapping-paper-size cardboard tube to store the finished rubbing. A stick of charcoal or large dark-colored crayon with the paper removed may be used as a rubbing stick.

Instruct students to tape the paper over the surface and to use the broad edge of the rubbing stick to make smooth, uniform strokes. Make sure all the detail has been rubbed before removing the paper. If charcoal is used, spray the image with a fixative to prevent smudging of the image. I have found it helpful to demonstrate the techniques of making a rubbing at the site.

8. Set the tone for your visit by emphasizing to students the solemnity of a cemetery. Remind them to show respect by acting in a dignified way, walking on paths provided, and working quietly. Do not move or disturb flowers or markers. Caution students to be aware of older stones that may be sinking or crumbling.

9. Present your students with a copy of "On-Site Activities for Cemetery Exploration." Divide the class into small groups and set time limits. I recommend no more than four to a group. My students usually work with a partner. Have students find and record answers to each of the questions on the handout. Be sure that students record their answers as some of the data will be used later for analysis in the classroom.

Wrap-Up

The following culminating activities are designed to be used after the cemetery visit. They include whole class as well as individual projects.

Have students evaluate and share the findings of their graveyard explorations. Ask what conclusions or inferences can be made from this cemetery study. Challenge your students to seek answers to unresolved questions.

Using information obtained at the cemetery, make bar graphs, line graphs, or picture graphics to express demographic information obtained.

Assign students to interview older family members about their ancestors. Tape record the interviews. Transfer the information to ancestry charts. Use this data to begin to develop a family tree.

Have students write historical fiction based on data collected at the cemetery. Create a class booklet and place it in the school library.

Study the burial rituals of various cultures. Have students report of the similarities and differences among rituals both among and within various cultures.

Have students memorize and present selections from the 244 poetic epitaphs in *Spoon River Anthology* (Masters, 1964) for a dramatic presentation. The follow is a list of epitaphs from Masters' *Spoon River Anthology* that I have had my students present in class.

- **Opening**
    The Hill (choral reading)

- **Scene I**
    Chase Henry
    Judge Somers
    Hannah Armstrong
    Seth Compton
    Lucinda Matlock

- **Scene II**
    "Indignation" Jones
    Mrs. George Reese
    Fiddler Jones
    Henry Phipps
    Lois Spears

- **Scene III**
    Louise Smith
    Isaiah Beethoven
    Emily Sparks
    Mrs. Kessler
    Josiah Tompkins

- **Scene IV**
    Blind Jack
    Mrs. Williams
    Dora Williams
    Rebecca Wasson

This activity is an appropriate and creative culmination to a cemetery study as the citizens of Spoon River who lie under the gray stones upon The Hill speak of their lives.

This cemetery activity is an excellent enrichment activity for any classroom.

Myra Weatherly taught many years in the public schools. She is now retired and devotes her time to writing.

Works Cited

Cooney, C. B. (1979). *Safe as the grave*. New York: Coward, McCann, and Geoghegan.

Gray, T. (1987). *Elegy written in a country churchyard*. New York: Chelsea House Publishers.

Masters, E. L. (1964). *A spoon river anthology*. New York: McMillan.

Schaefer, L. S. (1990). *Best of gravestone humor*. New York: Sterling Publishing Co.

On-Site Activities
For Cemetery Exploration

1. Begin the cemetery search by finding many different tombstone shapes. Draw at least six shapes and label them. Example: round, rectangular, square, cone, sphere, and pyramid.

2. Find the grave of someone who lived to be more than 65. Sketch the tombstone.

3. Make a list of 10 people who lived to be more than 65. Record dates of birth and death.

4. Find the grave of someone who died very young (under 12). Draw the tombstone.

5. Record names of 10 persons who died young with dates of birth and death. Divide into 50 year time periods. During which time period did the most children die? Why?

6. Find a significant tombstone (oldest person, famous person, or most unusual). Sketch the tombstone.

7. Find the oldest gravestone in the cemetery. Record name and dates.

8. Find the newest gravestone. Record name and dates.

9. Find the tombstone of someone who served in the Civil War. It may be marked with a metal cross. Draw the tombstone. Include all information. How does this differ from markers of people who served in other wars?

10. Find the markers for an entire family. Examine the names, dates, and epitaphs. Reconstruct the family tree.

11. Copy at least 10 epitaphs. Choose the best, the funniest, and the saddest epitaphs. Label them by category.

12. Determine what materials were used for the gravestones. Tally the kinds of stones.

13. Estimate the number of markers, using a sampling method. Visually divide the area into sections. Count the number of markers in one section, and then multiply the sample number by the number of sections.

14. Gather information for classifying tombstones. Determine ways tombstones can be classified. Examples: size, shape, names, color, decades, marker material.

15. Copy 15 names from headstones (random search). Record birth and death dates and age at death. Tally the ages in 10 year groups.

16. Record ages at death of 15 men and 15 women. Find the average age of death for each group. Compare the average age at death for women with the average age at death for men. What conclusions can you draw?

17. Measure the largest markers. Compare the dates on these monuments. Using this data, infer who might have been the most important members of the community.

18. Choose a tombstone that is intriguing. Record all information on the stone to use for a creative writing exercise.

19. Take notes of the living things found in the cemetery. Identify the trees, plants, and animals.

20. Make a tombstone rubbing.

Encouraging Challenging Discussions
The Role Of Students During Discussions Promoting Higher-Level Thinking

By Joan Daniels & Dr. Anne Udall

*T*he authors participated in a two-year special project to increase the teaching of higher-level thinking in an intermediate magnet school. The first year, "Thinklab" was essentially a demonstration teaching model. Classrooms revolved into Thinklab twice weekly with their teachers. The Thinklab teacher, whose expertise was formerly limited to Gifted and Talented students, taught lessons to entire classes.

The next year the model and philosophy changed considerably. The name was changed to "Creating The Thoughtful Classroom," and the responsibility was placed on the classroom teacher to create and deliver the lessons. Under this new structure, the Thinklab teacher acted as a staff development instructor and facilitator of a peer-coaching model. The purpose was to develop a collaboration among thinking teachers who designed and delivered higher-level thinking lessons.

A variety of information came from those years. The experiences generated the book Creating the Thoughtful Classroom *co-authored by Anne J. Udall and Joan Daniels. The role of the student in the thoughtful classroom was an issue explored. This article shares a few techniques used to formalize that role.*

What is it that every good classroom teacher does to "make it happen" in a higher-level thinking discussion? Researchers go into classrooms and code behaviors, tally words, count gestures, and measure personal distances, to find out what really makes certain teachers better at leading classroom discussions than others. Observing a great lesson is like watching a finely crafted movie. It flows, it "follows," it has an introduction, a message, and it packs a lasting impression. Is it in the directing? Is it the cast? Is it in the script? Or is it in the interaction and the chemistry generated by all three?

Everyday, in thousands of classrooms, teachers direct a kind of movie. They choose the script, and engage the actors. Yet, unlike a movie director, the teacher's purpose is not to entertain a passive audience, but to enlighten an active cast. They want the participants to leave with an enriched view of an idea or some new insight. The cast's active participation is vital.

The thoughtful classroom discussion has much in common with

a theatrical production. But the play we analogize is not the strictly-scripted one that may initially come to your mind. The production described does not have an enforced script. It is a higher-level thinking discussion of any topic in any thoughtful classroom. It is characterized by improvisation, by character insights, by embellishment, by creativity, and by its enrichment on the theme. Several different casts may play it out. Each time, they discover new insights and contribute in their unique way. The teacher's role is as director, disciplinarian, task-setter, questioner, antagonist, protagonist, encourager, and facilitator.

Setting the Stage

Setting the stage is very important. This entourage must work together for an extended period, and certain ground rules generally apply. But the classroom is a special stage with a unique cast. The cast is always young, often vulnerable, and sometimes unruly. The director must be firm, fair, and purposeful.

The truly higher-level thinking lesson is time-consuming to prepare, time-consuming to deliver, and important to evaluate. It is often in the form of a classroom discussion. A thoughtful discussion between two people can be an interactive challenge. A higher-level thinking discussion among twenty-five or more people with one leader is an educational feat. Because it requires the cooperative effort of so many bodies and minds, roles must be defined and rules must be followed.

It is important to note in this theatrical analogy that the teacher's role, like the director's, is minimized during the delivery. The best director has done all the work ahead. They simply initiate and guide the production. Teachers, of course, can not stand entirely aside once the lesson begins, but a good higher-level thinking discussion is characterized by few teacher comments. Therein lies the fundamental difference between a thoughtful discussion and a thoughtful lecture.

"Clueing In" The Cast

Good teachers have techniques and skills that facilitate the teaching of higher-level thinking activities. Those skills are not the subject of this article. What we would like to share is a way for the teacher to "clue in the cast." Sometimes, as teachers try to deliver the "perfect" lesson, they forget that the students have a responsibility in the endeavor. More often teachers realize the reciprocity of the thoughtful discussion, but neglect to notify students that they too have a role.

Roles and rules are often invisible in the room—that's what keeps the researches so busy tallying, coding, measuring, and hunting. Parameters are generally set up very early in the year, and, for better or worse, they set the stage for the remaining nine months.

We suggest that you post the expectations, review the rules, and discuss the roles. What our project taught us was that students did not carry around a set of rules for involvement in thoughtful discourse. They have learned "to play the game" but feel little responsibility to engage themselves honestly in an attempt to think. They have developed a wonderful arsenal to avoid thinking.

The Responsibilities Of The Cast

Student Behaviors That Interfere
With Thoughtful Discussions

It is amusing as well as insightful to have a look at behaviors that occur in the classroom that interfere with a thoughtful discussion. The "Matching Test" (see page 13), reproduced here for classroom use, is a tool we have employed to discuss the behaviors that interfere with a group's ability to discuss a topic thoughtfully. Total honesty will find teachers also reflecting back on their school days and seeing themselves as Harry Howsyrwife or Candy Cutesey. We all "drift" in difficult discussion tasks, and we've all contributed (or "dis-contributed") in like ways. Exploring these behaviors can help students recognize when they are drifting off task.

When presented with the matching sheet, students in the magnet school project quickly elaborated the student behaviors to teacher behaviors that interfered with a thoughtful discussion. Sixth-grade students were clearly aware of the dynamics involved in the classroom delivery of lessons. It was rather alarming to note that their comments were characterized by a competitive edge—teacher versus student. It became increasingly clear that students needed to see themselves as equally responsible for learning.

It is necessary to articulate a set of behaviors expected of the students. Some of the behaviors are overt some are not. Some can be evaluated, some cannot. They need a more specific direction than "Think!"

Student Behaviors Which Contribute
To The Thoughtful Discussion

Students develop habits of participation. If we don't want our students to continue old, familiar, non-thoughtful patterns we must initiate behavior change. There are nine behaviors students in the thoughtful classroom discussion must demonstrate. These need to be articulated, listed, followed, and evaluated.

The student will:

- participate
- give reasons for answers
- use precise, specific words
- take time to think about the problem and be comfortable with the amount of time a discussion takes
- stick with a problem, even though it is difficult
- offer different answers to one problem
- listen to what other students say
- think about his or her thinking
- ask complex-thinking questions about the topic

Students need to know that they are active participants and that the teacher-director has specific expectations.

A lesson hard-learned from the project was that these nine behaviors need to be tackled one at a time. They needed to be visually available (written on the board) and reiterated at each lesson.

Student Self-Evaluation

By the time students arrive at middle school, they have been exposed to many teaching styles. They have most likely experienced thoughtful classrooms and not-so-thoughtful ones. They have become a "consumer" of the educational cuisine. As a result, each student brings to a new classroom a set of behaviors and predispositions unique to his or her experiences.

The Self-Evaluation Form (see page 14), reproduced here is a mechanism for students to begin to analyze what they bring to a thoughtful classroom. We designed the form so that the odd numbered statements are more positive and the even are more negative. Students can compute and evaluate how negative or positive they are toward intellectual classroom pursuits.

The creative teacher will find many uses for this form.

- Tally the most common negative reactions: This gives the teacher empathy for the students. It can give the students insight into themselves.

- Tally the most common positive reactions: The teacher will gain insights into the strengths and preferences of the class.
- Use information from the tallies with the class to brainstorm solutions to student concerns during discussions.
- Use it again at the end of the year for post-test evaluation.

The Student Self-Evaluation Lesson (this page) needs to be used periodically by students for their own growth and to provide feedback to the teacher. Unless the teacher specifically states ahead, these self-evaluation forms need to remain a private affair.

Summary

Experience in the Creating the Thoughtful Classroom project has taught us important things about assisting students in their roles. The role of the student in the thoughtful classroom is vital. It needs articulation. We can no longer assume that students have accumulated the skills necessary to participate in thoughtful discussions by virtue of their participation in the educational system. Specific behaviors must be discussed, posted, and evaluated. "Listen to what Others Say" must not be trivialized or assumed by teachers.

Just a few ideas are presented here. Creative teachers will add and elaborate. A fuller description of the project and the resulting evaluation forms and teaching strategies is available in the book, Creating the Thoughtful Classroom. *The book can be obtained from Zephyr Press, P.O. Box 13448, Tucson, AZ 85732-3448; (602) 322-5090.*